OUTSTANDING! Jim, you have done it again! You practiced what you preached. You told me, "I want to write a book! All I need to do is jump in and start swimming!"

The interesting and poignant stories you share to support your values, beliefs, and actions for success are superb. Anyone can benefit by escaping into your life's adventures. They will take to heart the underlying elements you learned through your journey of "plunging in."

You write as you speak, making for an easy read with powerful, positive, actionable, and vital elements for being successful in any path in life.

Steve Gesing
Former National Director; Executive VP, Smith Barney
Consulting Group; Former Senior Divisional Sales Director,
MFS Private Portfolio Services; Current Owner, CEO and
Area Developer, CMIT Solutions of The Merrimack Valley

I enjoyed it; it was almost like [Naughton was] telling me the story over a few drinks. I especially liked his "bullet" points in Chapter 12. They are sound advice for anyone in any profession at any point in their career. I had a basic understanding of how mutual funds work, and this book considerably enhanced that knowledge.

Steve Paglarini
U.S. Department of the Treasury

I first met Jim nearly 25 years ago, and I was immediately struck by his honesty and humility. So writing a book that might have felt almost boastful must have been extremely difficult for him. But how can a successful man tell his truth without imparting some success stories?

Jim's greatest point is that "showing up" is 90% of being successful; working long hours and being a student of your given profession makes up the rest!

Gary Venable
First Vice President, Merrill Lynch

Jump In
and
Start Swimming

A Story of the Unique,

Lucrative Career and Life of a

Billion-Dollar Wholesaler

James P. Naughton

KEY
Publishing Company

Jump In and Start Swimming

ISBN 978-0-615-52816-8

© 2012 by James P. Naughton
Key Publishing Company

JP Naughton Sales Performance Company

www.KeysForSellingSuccess.com

LinkedIn

Facebook

Printed in the United States of America

Cover design by John Morris-Reihl—www.artntech.com

Author picture on back cover: Soozie Sundlun of East Greenwich
Photo & Studio (www.egphoto.com, www.egphotoweddings.com)

Book editing, layout, and design by
Martha Nichols/aMuse Productions®

To my wife

Sharon Maureen McCarthy Naughton

Thank you for your love, your support, and sacrifices.

Because of you, I was successful, and our family thrived.

Happy 40th anniversary—August 21, 2012—to us both.

ACKNOWLEDGMENTS

I believe that service is the cement of relationships. I also believe that communication is a major part of the backbone of any successful business. To my mind, Dale Carnegie provides the best communication training in the world. I am a graduate, as are Warren Buffet and many other famous individuals. My success speaks for itself, and of course everyone knows of Warren Buffet. In this very competitive job market, one needs to set oneself apart from the masses! Whatever your niche in life, I urge you to look into Dale Carnegie Training (for greater Boston, New Hampshire, Maine, and Rhode Island, contact John MacKinnon, Performance Training Associates; office 781.894. 2700, ext. 233; cell 781.254.8585; other locales, see www.dale-carnegie.com).

Special thanks to my childhood friend John Choquette, who decided along with me to nervously leave our great blue-collar jobs to follow our friend Jim Maloney and enroll in college as full-time students. John and I motivated each other to continue and eventually graduate, albeit a little older than the usual grad. Thanks to John for his life advice and input for my book. John joined me when I jumped in and started swimming.

Thank you to my friend Alger Mitchell, who often performed on Newport, Rhode Island's famous waterfront at Christie's Restaurant and thoroughly entertained my clients during the 1990s. Even Jim Brinkley, former vice chairman of Legg Mason, was an Alger fan. He showed up as Alger was releasing a new CD, and I had Alger autograph Jim's copy.

Thank you to Arthur, graphic designer, Denise, manager, and Raoul Holzinger, president of Print World (on Post Road, North Kingstown, Rhode Island).They helped with all my early marketing campaigns and, most recently, formatting pictures for this book, including the collages.

Special thanks to my 5th-grade buddy Bill White. He and I recall our early years (and much much more!) each time we meet at Paddy's at Misquamicut Beach in Westerly, Rhode Island. Thanks, Bill, for helping me to stay grounded.

Thanks to Dan Bruce for his proofreading and all his hard work (Daniel Bruce, Stylus Editing, www.stylusediting.com, 802.839.9067, Daniel@stylusediting.com).

Thanks also to John Morris-Reihl (www.artntech.com) for his beautiful cover and to Martha Nichols (aMuse Productions®) for her help in designing, editing, and laying out this book.

TABLE OF CONTENTS

FOREWORD

S oon after my short-lived retirement from the financial services industry, a friend suggested that I participate in his
class at the University of Rhode Island. Mark Crevier, recently
retired CEO of Kent County Hospital, began teaching a course at
URI, providing students with a real-life look at careers, inter-
views, and more. At first a noncredit elective, it has evolved to
become a mandatory course for seniors. In preparation for my
visit to his class I began to write down some memoirs of my career. Unexpectedly, the words and experiences just came pouring out of my head, and it appeared that instead of writing a
speech—I had the makings of a book.

In addition to Mark's request, I have a few additional inten-
tions in writing this book:

- First, I plan to introduce college seniors and recent graduates to a unique sales career; that of a financial wholesaler—
  a career I first learned of in 1980.

- Second, I am hoping my life experiences—growing up in a
  housing project with my younger sister Kathleen and beautiful, loving parents James and Julia Naughton, who through
  life's circumstances left their native homeland with only a
  fourth-grade education—might inspire and motivate students, the unemployed, and anyone who might benefit from
  my life and work experiences.

- Third, I want to provide some history of the early days of financial wholesaling for new wholesalers while at the same

time offering a tribute to the stockbrokers, the financial advisors who would make my success possible.

- Fourth, and most important for me, is to leave this book as a memoir to my fantastic grandchildren—Jack, age 8; twins Sam and Cole Naughton, age 7—and any more that my wife Sharon and I might be blessed with.

- In addition, I want to acknowledge my loving and supportive wife Sharon; my eldest son Tim and his wife Cristina, parents of our grandchildren; our middle son Matthew; and our daughter Erin. As a result, while this book contains primarily information and stories of my business career, it also contains some of my personal life experiences along with a few personal pictures in the Appendix.

I have been "there"—and without having the IQ or SAT scores of the president of the United States or other famous CEOs. I grew up in the projects with hard-working parents who didn't have the education to provide me with the vocabulary or career planning advice that any teenager facing adulthood needs. I grew up poor and began dropping out of school, but thanks to God, my parents, and friends I pulled myself up. It took awhile: I was 27 when I finally graduated from college despite the fact that I was initially refused acceptance into *any* program because of my low SAT scores.

Please note, this book is not saying that college is a prerequisite to success. Rather, it is to motivate you to be the best that you can. Pick a goal or goals, write them down, and file them away. With goals and faith, anything is possible. As I was growing up, my mother would often repeat, "Jimmy, just jump in and start swimming!" Books like *The Secret* or *Rich Dad, Poor Dad* are excellent reading.

Visualization has been key throughout the ages. However, for some, the techniques take too long and eventually action is required. Often it's *any* action. You can listen to motivational speakers on CDs, and you probably *should*, if for no other reason than to drown out the negativity that constantly bombards us.

Sometimes however, motivational speakers can get a listener all pent up with nowhere to go. Imagine yourself at the edge of the Amazon River, and suddenly you are surrounded by a headhunting tribe. What would you do? Right—you would "jump in and start swimming!" Remember the story of Moses in the Bible, with the Israelites being pursued by the Egyptians? They jumped in—to the Red Sea! In either situation, books like *The Secret* would not have saved you—there isn't always enough time. You can sit around and think positive thoughts all you want, but eventually you have to get up off the chair and do something!

You and I are here for a reason. If you are doubtful...just do it. Some call this faith. You have nothing to lose; proceed anyway. And how do you really know what you want to do in life unless you give it a try? People have ideas, skills, and talents, but often lack the energy to "just do it." Most often in life, you won't get the energy until you take the first step and do something; it's then that you learn one of life's mysterious secrets, which is "Once you force yourself to do something, that's when the energy comes!" My beautiful mother Julia made it to sixth grade before leaving school to help with the family farm in Ireland; I hope you will agree with me that her "jump in and start swimming" saying is worthy of consideration.

One of my closest friends owns Irving Shechtman & Co., Inc., one of the largest and most successful auction companies in New England. Skip Ponte didn't finish high school, let alone college, but was still extremely successful. Another friend, John Petrella, grew up in a working-class neighborhood of Providence, Rhode Island raised by a single parent and a few aunts. John became one of the highest ranking members in the Department of Treasury's Internal Revenue Service.

Still another friend is David Milbury, who brought me into his firm and mentored my career. Dave came from a blue-collar neighborhood just outside Boston. He also became a senior vice president in a famous mutual fund company, and set all kinds of sales records. Later on in this book you will see what a friend, teacher, mentor, and boss he became. Dave has had a profound affect on my career and life.

I intend this book to encourage learning more about sales, as I have found that people are selling their entire lives—whether it's selling a future employer on one's capabilities or selling a bank loan officer on giving a loan or mortgage. (By the way, what do you think Skip does in his auction company? Right—he sells!) I will also introduce you to a career that is relatively unknown outside the financial services industry—that of a financial wholesaler. My plan is to help you find an entry-level position, if this career appeals to you. My website is www.KeysForSell-ingSuccess.com, and I am on LinkedIn and Facebook as well.

Finally, I have had the pleasure of working with a couple thousand financial advisors, stockbrokers, and managers over a 30-year span as a financial wholesaler in all of the notable wire-house firms, including Dean Witter (now Morgan Stanley), Merrill Lynch, Smith Barney (now merged with Morgan Stanley), A.G. Edwards and First Albany (now merged with Wells Fargo), Janney Montgomery Scott, LPL, and others. This book will finally allow them to know what I did after breakfast or lunch meetings. My sincere thanks to them for their business and for the memories; without them, I couldn't have brought in more than $3 billion in sales, including close to $1 billion in a single year.

In addition I spent approximately ten years in various careers within the insurance industry, representing firms like The Travelers, Aetna, and Metropolitan. I sold directly door to door and through insurance brokers and held positions as an insurance sales consultant–trainer to hundreds of insurance salesmen. These individuals sell products that protect your loved ones and your estates. Now it's time for you, the reader, the recent graduate, the future graduate, or the currently unemployed, to "Jump in and start swimming!"

INTRODUCTION

THE BEGINNING

He sat alone in a holding cell in the main processing building on Ellis Island. It was winter, one of the coldest in more than 50 years. It was 1930, and waves of immigrants were making their way to Ellis Island. The surroundings reminded him of the jail cell he had escaped from in Castlebar, County Mayo, almost a year earlier. Immigrants needed to have someone "claim" them when—and if—they passed a myriad of examinations and tests. All of his buddies had been released to aunts and uncles hours before.

James Naughton, my father, waited and waited, disoriented, freezing, confused, and downtrodden, missing Ireland and his parents and siblings back on their small farm in Clooncurra just outside Castlebar. He was wondering what awaited him. Were the streets of New York really paved with gold? Where was his aunt? Was he going to be sent back to Liverpool? Lonely, he spent the night dozing on and off, dreaming, remembering pieces of the events that pushed, forced, and dragged him to America.

He and many of his childhood friends were members or pretended to be members of the IRA back home. It wasn't really a choice; it was survival. In the 1920s the parents of young English soldiers deemed duty in Ireland too dangerous for their sons, so they pressured the English Parliament to do something. Parliament came up with a brilliant idea—why not release from prisons some thousands of criminals and thugs, along with other troublemakers who should have been in prison but weren't, and allow them to "police" the Irish? This is what my father and his neighbors believed; however, it appears that many of the Black and Tans were out-of-work veterans of other wars. They were given some minimal training and provided them with special uniforms; the uniform colors gave these thugs their infamous name, the Black and Tans. It's no secret that this group terrorized the local farmers; they were downright brutal and would beat them mercilessly.

A band of Black and Tans roughed up and nearly killed one of my father's neighbors. He apparently was an older farmer and didn't have sons to help him. Later the body of a Black and Tan was discovered in a local turf bog. Without any questioning or proof, they immediately rounded up any young male farmers suspected of being members of the IRA and put them in jail in Castlebar—including my father.

My father's mother—my grandmother—Mariah, walked to town barefoot with her black European dress and shawl and conducted a hunger strike, sleeping on the damp, cold cobblestones. After several days without food and with little sleep, my grandmother, nearly exhausted from her pleadings to the authorities, noticed a local priest being admitted to the jail. She begged and pleaded for the release of her son. The priest suggested she go home retrieve some of Dad's clothes and wait for his signal.

Together, the priest and my grandmother were allowed to enter the jail for a private meeting and confession with my father. When they left, my father was wearing the priest's tunic and hat. The priest lay covered up in the cot. Our understanding was that the priest convinced the guards that he was knocked out and his clothes were stolen. My father was smuggled to Dublin, placed on a fishing trawler, and dropped off with relatives living in Liverpool, England. Liverpool was home to a lot of Irish. Later he got on a German ship and made his way to New York.

His aunt finally showed up 30 hours later and signed a paper, and he was allowed to leave for Manhattan with his burlap bag to collect the gold nuggets that he believed lined the streets of New York. His aunt simply abandoned him. In a few hours, he entered a bread line in the Battery section of Manhattan and stayed there for almost six months while looking for any type of work.

Did he have anything to do with the killing of the Black and Tan? He told me that while he hated them and might rough them up a bit, to kill another human being would be impossible.

The following is mere speculation regarding the priest. My father's brother John was a priest, or soon to be ordained. We're not sure of the details, but he mysteriously left the priesthood and showed up in New York. He made his way to San Francisco to find gold and was apparently killed. There is a question as to whether he may have been the one who helped my father escape.

When my father finally found a construction job in the Bronx, gangs would show up each payday, usually a Friday, to collect their "protection fee." He flashed some sort of insignia or badge that had to do with the IRA, and he was left alone. He felt that as crazy as the mobsters were, they weren't crazy enough to mess with the IRA. He watched fellow laborers resist the extortion only to be hit on the head with a shovel and buried immediately, in with the concrete, to become part of the streets of New York. As he said, it was not only the time of the Great Depression but also a lawless time.

THE GREAT DEPRESSION

On his fourth Sunday at Mass, my father and his buddies were listening to the priest stating that "my dear brethren, we are experiencing our coldest winter in 50 to 100 years. *[This mention of the cold winter was also in a line from the movie "Cinderella Man"—a film about the era.]* Many of you have no jobs, so please, we don't want any more of your buttons!" You see, the Irish immigrants were brought up in the old country to put

1. Coastal view of my parents' homeland, County Mayo, Ireland.

2. SS Cleveland steamship, believed to be the ship my father sailed on from Liverpool to the USA.

3. Statue of Liberty. She welcomed him and thousands of immigrants from all over the world.

4. Ellis Island, where immigrants were inspected and accepted or rejected.

5. Dad's first view of the Manhattan skyline (modern-day version).

6. Dad stood in the breadlines of the Great Depression.

7. My beautiful mother Julia holding me in the United Homes Housing Project. Note the wooden sidewalks —tar and oil-base products were needed for the war.

8. The Hartford Times building. My first job—and my first sales job—was newspaper delivery boy.

9. The United Aircraft Federal Credit Union—my first after-school job.

10. Electric power linesman—my first career.

11. Central Connecticut State University— graduated in 1970.

12. The Travelers Insurance Company—first sales career out of college.

13. Metropolitan Life Insurance Company—sales consultant and trainer.

14. Dean Witter Reynolds—First Wall Street career.

15. Massachusetts Financial Services—Regional Vice President and Billion Dollar Wholesaler.

a penny in the collection basket. Out of embarrassment for not having a penny, they began ripping the buttons off of their overcoats and tossing those in the basket instead. Often, during my wholesaling career, when the stock market occasionally tanked or we went into a recession, I would tell my brokers, "Remember the buttons" to get them to realize that the current situation was nothing compared to the 1930s.

When my children would ask me if that could ever happen again, I told them that in those times, one of every five Americans were farmers, there was a dustbowl in the middle of the country, and back then we didn't have Social Security or government oversight agencies (such as the SEC) until 1933. There was no FINRA and no FDIC, nor did they have unemployment insurance. I ended with authority: "So, no, we could not have another Great Depression."

I was *so* wrong!

It's not exactly the same because of what I just mentioned, but we have had—at least for many Americans—a second Great Depression. I also forgot about the "Greed Factor" and the devastation that greed can cause. We more than sampled it in 2008. It's not the Great Depression, but these are hard times, too, and a lot of folks are hurting—and a lot of high school and college graduates are having difficulty finding employment. I hope my story—the year I graduated, 1970, provided a *terrible* job market—and my unique sales career will give some help to you and anyone else who needs encouragement, ideas, or just a job.

MINI-BIOGRAPHY

I was born in Hartford, Connecticut, during the 1940s to James and Julia Naughton, both of whom emigrated from Ireland. As previously mentioned, Dad arrived on Ellis Island around 1930 amongst one of the last waves of Irish immigrants. My mother came a little later and was "claimed" by a wealthy Jewish family of international importers. My parents met and married in Manhattan and later found jobs at Pratt & Whitney Aircraft and relocated to East Hartford, Connecticut.

My father would often to say to me with his brogue as I was growing up, "Jimmy me lad, I love me native country, but no place in the world compares to America. You have a freedom here to do and accomplish anything you put your mind to." I am not a zillionaire, but I listened to him and have had many successes. Thank you, Dad; thank you, Mom!

The United Homes housing project located in East Hartford, Connecticut, was a war housing project set up for the employees of Pratt & Whitney Aircraft where both my parents began working after leaving New York City. The homes were tiny, one-bedroom and two-bedroom with no insulation—the wall on the inside was the same wall you saw on the outside. A single central kerosene heater provided the heat. In the summer, it was like living in an attic; fans were not plentiful, but as a kid you had no knowledge of anything better, so this was your home and you felt safe.

There were at least 50 to 70 kids living in close proximity. We always had something to do: army games, sandlot ball games,

View of the United Homes housing project, East Hartford, Connecticut; 1950s.

My father, James Naughton, holding yours truly. United Homes.

My younger sister Kathleen and me in front of our one-story apartment. United Homes.

kid games, and lots of fun—what a way for a kid to develop his imagination! I now look back at the time when my children were growing up—watching all three of them in playing in a bunch of organized sports and now attending games with my grandchildren—and thinking that in my era, living in the projects was not all that bad. There are projects, and there are projects. This project was one of the better ones; however, if you weren't tough, you learned to become tough quickly. Even if you didn't win a battle, you made sure that the neighborhood bullies thought twice about coming back at you a second time. I could write a book on the experience of growing up in the United Homes Project alone, but suffice it to say that the experience prepared me for the future. I will discuss many facets of my sales career in this book, but let's just say starting out that one has to be tough to make it in sales.

My parents worked very hard and saved enough money to buy our first home, about half a mile way. There was also a paper route available, so in 1954 at age nine I began my first sales job, delivering newspapers for the *Hartford Times*. In those days you delivered papers, collected the money on weekends, and constantly tried to bring in or sell new customers, touting the qualities of the news-paper and your services as a paperboy. Later on, the newspaper industry followed an evolution into telemarketing for new customers, which is how yours truly ended up managing the number one newspaper telemarketing operation in the United States.

I was a paperboy until age 15, and then I took a job at the Lobster Trap fish restaurant around the corner from my house, selling lobsters and washing dishes—you name it, I did it. When I turned 16, I landed a job at the United Aircraft Federal Credit Union, which at the time was the largest such federal credit union in the U.S. It was at the corner entrance of my street. After school from 3 P.M. to 6 P.M. and on Saturday mornings, I cut the grass, filed folders, went on errands, sent client statements...I did everything! Unfortunately, it eliminated the possibility of playing high school sports (although realistically, we didn't have a car, and the school was quite a distance from my house, and as a family we still couldn't spend frivolously). Even with all the jobs, I managed to have a load of friends, and we had a generally fun time. We played lots of softball and sandlot football (with no helmets) and also rode our Schwinn bicycles without helmets. I did okay in high school; however, the after-school jobs took a huge toll on my studies.

We moved from the projects in 1956. My parents—who once stood in bread lines in the Battery section of Manhattan, 3,000 miles from their families, with no cell phones or anyone to help them—had saved enough from their jobs at Pratt Whitney and other part-time work to purchase *for cash* a decent home on Colt Street.

One street over from our house lived a boy a year older than me, Johnny Sullivan, whose father was a mailman. Johnny lived with his family in a small rented apartment. He did finish high school, but instead of going to college, he got a job as a repairman for a company called Addressograph Multigraph. One night while we were all out partying, Pratt & Whitney needed service at 1:00 A.M. As their usual serviceman was unavailable, they somehow located Johnny, who left us to help Pratt & Whitney.

The rest was history: Pratt & Whitney took a liking to Johnny and asked that he be assigned as their permanent repairman. Soon a sales position opened up, and Johnny threw his hat in the ring with a lot of college graduates. Not only did he get the job by the early 1970s, but he also became president of the firm before turning 30 and easily took to the life of a CEO with private jets, etc. I last saw him in Newport celebrating the purchase of an historic Newport mansion.

Next is John Larson who, like me, grew up in a housing project, also in East Hartford, with a bunch of siblings—although his project, Mayberry Village, was considered a little higher-end than ours. Initially because of a 5- or 6-year age difference, I didn't know John while we were growing up. In fact, it wasn't until years later that I learned we had both graduated from Central

Connecticut State College (now CCSU, a university) in 1971. I actually finished in June 1970, but my diploma says 1971.

Incidentally, the tuition was $90 per semester. That's right, I didn't say $9,000 or $90,000; I said *ninety dollars*. Per semester. Incredible! You might recognize John as a recent guest of MSNBC's Andrea Mitchell Show. John is (currently) a senior Congressman from Connecticut.

By the way, one of our classmates at CCSU, Carol Ammon (1973), is Chairman of the Board of a major health corporation. She just donated the largest gift to CCSU ever—$8 million. (Remember the $90 per semester?) I mention that just in case you think that because you didn't graduate from Harvard, you might not land the job or career of your dreams. My experience has shown me it's all up to you: I (and others) can provide insight and guidance, but *you* have to *discern*!!

Like me, all of these guys (I exclude Carol Ammon here because I do not know her background) could have gone in other directions: gangs, drugs, mediocrity. But they didn't. Why? Their stories are wide and varied and probably more impressive than mine. However, I still did something big, and in discussing it, maybe I will help you. You might not choose sales or wholesaling as a career. Maybe you will enter the new green energy industry. Green energy is attractive particularly because, as with wholesaling back in the 1970s and 80s, very few people are yet aware of the opportunity.

Anyway, I enlisted in the United States Marine Corps Reserves in 1963. It was a five-year commitment, and considering that we were not at war (at least, none that we knew of), it seemed like a better alternative for serving my country than taking my chances with the draft. It also allowed me to eventually attend college. I did my basic training at Parris Island beginning in January 1964 and finished active duty that summer, which was when I came to realize that all hell was breaking loose in a country called Vietnam.

I began evening classes at the University of Hartford and then began working for the Hartford Electric Light & Power Company

(HELCO). I eventually worked my way up to "C" linesman. It's hard to believe, as I now nervously climb up a 4-foot stepladder, that I once climbed 40-foot poles with a pair of hooks and a belt so I could work on live wires. At that time, HELCO was probably the best-paying blue-collar job in America. They had unlimited benefits and paid 100% of their employees" education, which I took advantage of.

Meanwhile, the Reserves were "on again, off again" with stand-by alerts for Vietnam, although we were never activated. Many of us were naïvely disappointed; but it just wasn't meant to be. During our monthly weekend drills at the Reserve Center, it took a number of Purple Heart Award ceremonies for the parents of fallen Marines for us to finally grasp what was going on in this place called Vietnam.

I continued with college at night and finally decided to matriculate as a full-time student. This decision was aided by the death of one of HELCO's senior line foremen in a freak accident. He had been trying to do everyone a favor so that we could head back to headquarters more quickly, but unfortunately, he died immediately when a gust of wind blew the dead wire we were running up against a live 13kV wire at the same time the he was pulling up a grounding pole.

College was a whirlwind experience for me. My initial anxiety about my age versus the other students (I was 23 while most were 17 to 21) soon was mitigated as the returning Vietnam vets began pouring into college. I worked at night for the American Automobile Association (AAA) as a dispatcher. I was able to study while working this job. Because of my age and Marine Corps active duty time, I was able to substitute teach in East Hartford Elementary and High School, and I was also an on-call beer delivery assistant for the East Hartford Budweiser franchise.

I was able to manage these part-time jobs because I would load up my classes on Tuesdays and Thursdays. Please don't think I recommend this workload in either college or high school, but sometimes you just do what you have to do. In spite of the work, I was able to join a veteran's fraternity. As it turned out, guys that I hadn't seen in years were returning from Vietnam and attending college on the G.I. bill. I traveled with them to Florida during spring break and with the college alumni to Germany during winter break. I was given a free cruise vacation by the travel division of the Hartford AAA and participated in all the fraternity parties and dances.

It was while I was in college that I became acquainted with tapes such as "The Strangest Secret" by Earl Nightingale and such books as *Think and Grow Rich* by Napoleon Hill. *Psycho-Cybernetics* by Dr. Maxwell Maltz offered ideas of success by using and focusing one's mind to achieve a goal. The book contains a story of the two British champion dart throwers and how they practiced and prepared so differently. One threw darts in a local pub for hours each day, and the other rented a house in the Scottish Highlands and imagined throwing bull's-eyes in an imaginary circle on a white cloth for hours at a time. Who won, the one who physically threw darts all day or the one who used his mind and imagination? You guessed it: The latter won. There are many such examples of individuals using their minds to achieve goals.

One weekend during summer 1969, I decided to take a break and travel with a friend to a dude ranch in upstate New York. Due to some misdirection, we found ourselves in a small town called Woodstock on a rainy Friday evening.

You can read about what I refer to as my "Forrest Gump" Woodstock adventure on the "Articles" page of my website, www.KeysForSellingSuccess.com.

I graduated in 1970 with a B.A. in English and a minor in psychology (I had planned on a teaching career). When a professor asked me what I was going to do, I said that I wasn't quite sure, but I "knew I was going to earn a lot of money." However, 1970 turned out to be a difficult time to find any job. While not as bad as today, it took me from June 1970 until mid-January 1971 to find one. What did I do while waiting? I found a job as a carpenter's helper on Cape Cod. We—an ex-steeple jack in the witness protection program, another college kid, and me—built a two-story electrical supply building. Yes, it's still standing on Higgins Crowell Road in Yarmouth, Massachusetts.

I mention all of these different jobs with hope of creating and pointing out as many job opportunities as possible during these difficult times. Feel free to contact me via my website if you need more ideas. I have had more part-time jobs than I have listed here, and temporary employment might help you pay the bills while you seek a career.

Finally, eight months later I was accepted as a Group Insurance sales trainee for the Travelers Insurance Company in Hartford. It was an intense one-year training program in which I learned everything about the insurance business, not just "group insurance." I also received extensive training in sales, which carried over into all my future employment. This was where I first began to learn about sales and how to sell. It's also where I met my wife, Sharon, who was an assistant to a senior vice president at the Travelers. We have been married for 40 years and have three children and three grandchildren.

Upon completion of the training program, I was assigned to the Princeton/Trenton (New Jersey) Travelers office and began selling group insurance and pension products. Reminiscing, I realize now that I received some valuable experience for my future as a wholesaler because as a group insurance salesman, you're not selling direct to the customer—rather, you call on insurance brokerage houses like Johnson Higgins and Marsh Mac and sell through their representatives. During this period, I also took a part-time job selling men's and boys" clothes on the evenings and weekends. Soon I was selling more than anybody else, even full-time employees—however, I also made a lot of enemies and ticked off management as a result of my "aggressive" sales style and was fired.

It was a lesson I never forgot, because I realized being number one wasn't a guarantee of anything long term. Teamwork, getting along with fellow employees, and not soiling the merchandise was equally important. Soon I decided to relocate to Connecticut and worked as an insurance agent, eventually becoming a junior partner in an insurance agency. I continued to hone my selling skills, even attempting selling door-to-door. I realized quickly that selling door-to-door was not my forte.

You are probably starting to realize that in my quest for success I wasn't afraid to "roll up my shirt sleeves" and work hard. If that thought scares you, I would put the book down now and go back to being a shepherd or whatever puts a smile on your face.

Chapter One

BEGINNING MY WHOLESALING
CAREER—DECEMBER 1980

I n the mid-1970s, I was approached by MetLife to become a consultant and trainer working at their New England headquarters in Rhode Island. By that time I was well versed in all areas and lines of insurance and had a beginning knowledge of mutual funds. I was also gaining a reputation as a sales consultant. I taught a private selling skills course and also worked with the telephone company to develop telemarketing programs. I parlayed this experience at night by working for the *Providence Journal.*

You may remember that I started my sales career as a newspaper boy. The Providence Journal was extremely successful during that era in bringing in new customers. It ranked number one in the country for selling newspapers by telephone. I managed about 20 telemarketers Monday through Friday and Saturday mornings. The negative was that I generally had to fire two or three employees every Friday night who could not make their quota. I have always thought that most people could learn to be a salesman; however, I think good telemarketers are born with the knack. Toward the end of 1980, I was pretty much burned out with sometimes working three jobs.

In fall, a friend mentioned that a Wall Street firm by the name of Dean Witter Reynolds was looking for "an insurance guy." Eventually, I got in touch with their National Sales Manager for Annuities and Insurance, named Don Webber. Our discussion led to a meeting at the Boston DWR office with Don and the new Northeast District Director, Jim Dwyer. When they later called to offer me the job of Annuity Wholesaler for the Northeast, I "shrewdly" turned them down. I say "shrewdly" facetiously, since I was working three jobs at the time, one full-time and two part-time. But at the time, I had never traveled to any extent, had a young family, never worked for a Wall Street firm, and didn't know what wholesaling meant.

Jim Dwyer said, "Naughton, we're not going to let you make that decision until your interview at DWR headquarters at the World Trade Center."

I later told my wife Sharon that I felt like I was speaking to the mob. I mean, who were these guys telling me I couldn't make my own decision? The next morning I was on a flight to LaGuardia and then into Manhattan. Promptly at 9:00 A.M. at 5 World Trade Center, I met with the National Director of Annuity Sales, Tom Peck. Fifteen minutes later I was an employee of Dean Witter Reynolds.

A tongue-in cheek note to college seniors: Do not say no to a job offer unless you're 100% sure of your decision! I almost lost out, not only on a great career but on one that was to become a life-changing opportunity for me and my family. I tripled the income I was getting from three jobs in my first year. As you will see later, the first year was peanuts compared to what was to come.

Because many of my readers might have little knowledge of annuities, I believe it appropriate to provide some background. The annuity was and is an insurance product, and as a life insurance consultant, my experience with them was in the form of what is referred to as an "immediate annuity." You, as a client, might need a fixed income payable monthly for life or a certain period and beginning in a month. The insurance company's actuaries will calculate a number (payment) based on what the company can earn on your assets plus some other data.

In the late 1970s when the stock market was in the doldrums, a competitor firm known as E. F. Hutton decided to take a look at and develop products based on the "accumulation phase" component of the annuity. Sec. 72 is the IRS Code that allows money to accumulate on a compounded, tax-deferred basis. In the late 1970s to early 1980s, these annuities that became known as *single premium deferred annuities* often had interest rates much higher than taxable bank CDs, some paying 15% and higher. When you can compound these rates on a tax-deferred basis, you can easily begin to realize their appeal to investors who were getting very little out of the stock market.

Later on, variable products were introduced to allow investors to purchase the clones of mutual funds that allowed you to take advantage of the stock market on a tax-deferred basis as it began to explode in 1982. Today annuity wholesalers sell mostly variable annuities.

I met some incredible salesmen during my career with Dean Witter, and I learned from all of them—folks like Porter Pierpont Morgan (yes, of that famous family), one of the best public speakers I have ever met. Porter was offered a vice presidency at the American stock exchange and later with Liberty Financial. Early on, I probably borrowed most of my sales ideas from Milt Padowitz, a Florida wholesaler. He was one of those unique individuals who could spew out one sales idea after another, something I wouldn't witness again until years later with a wholesaler named K. David Milbury.

A word on fate, coincidences, etc. (and I probably will have more to say on it later on): Sometimes things are just meant to be. I believe now, years later, that I would have had to do something awful to all three of the above VPs in order not to get the job. In my bio, I mention how as a U.S. Marine Reservist my buddies and I naïvely petitioned our commander to be activated as a unit when the Vietnam War broke out, only to be told that they didn't activate reserves in an undeclared war, unlike today. I say naïvely, because at our young ages, we didn't have a clue.

Looking back, as a 3.5 Rocket Launcher Specialist, I probably would have had a 3- or 4-month life expectancy. I don't pretend to understand—except that, for some people, some things are just meant to be.

While working and growing, I must admit I never thought much about the subject, but as I began writing down my memoirs, so-called "coincidences" started to grab my interest. Recently I received a type of "new-age" email message from some unknown source. The very last sentence stated, "There are only coincidences when God remains anonymous." Interesting.

In contrast to today's practices, I had no training for wholesaling and minimal training in financial products initially. Like Warren Buffet, I became interested in Dale Carnegie and enrolled in a class at the Hartford, Connecticut, YMCA during the early 1970s. This was, and still is, one of the best courses in the art of communication in the world. Because I had to work many evenings, I could not complete the course until 30 years later, but I did read many of Carnegie's writings; which have had a tremendous positive effect on my life.

I got a brief personal introduction to managers in New England and upstate New York. December 1980 and the holidays came and went quickly. Things began to move even more quickly in January. I studied the products and called a number of senior colleagues for help and tips on working my territory.

My motto in life and the title of this book is a phrase that my mother often presented to me: "Jump in and start swimming!" And that I proceeded to do at DWR (Dean Witter Reynolds, now Morgan Stanley).

When I taught selling skills, the first step in the selling process was the Attention Phase. John "Mickey" Finn, our Georgia wholesaler and a transplant from Long Island, was an avid baseball fan. He turned his business card into a part baseball card, with a picture of him suited up, taken while he attended spring training (talk about attention getting). And I was astute enough to learn from others like John. I borrowed ideas from everyone who was successful and then added and blended them with my own.

Late in 1982, Don Johnson became National Sales Manager. Don learned quickly that I wasn't a big drinker. We were at happy hour at the Buffalo Hilton just before a dinner engagement at the exclusive Cloister Restaurant. Due to time constraints, we were forced to down our cabernet quickly, which I did. Unfortunately, when I got to the Cloisters, I actually slid down five steps into the main dining area. Earlier that evening during the hotel happy hour, I had had two glasses of wine, which was not really a lot. Sometimes your system, due to nerves, blood sugar level, etc., can wreak havoc—particularly if you're rushing to get to dinner.

Talk about a horror show—and during my first trip with our new National Sales Manager. Instead of firing me, he called a taxi to take me back to the Hilton. Don never mentioned the event again, and I learned to watch my alcohol intake. We all went on to even greater successes. Dean Witter is where and how I learned to wholesale. As I said, during my first year, I tripled my income from the previous twelve months, a not insignificant accomplishment, considering I had been working three jobs.

Sadly, Jim Dwyer passed in April 2006. Earlier that month, a mutual friend, John O'Neil, Manager of Morgan Stanley in Greenwich, Connecticut, and also a Jim Dwyer hire, called me and helped to arrange a reunion conference call with Jim. I remarked to my wife that he sounded strong, witty, like his old self. He passed away two weeks later.

Jim supported me in everything I did in those early years. I did have the opportunity to speak with and extend my condolences to his son Patrick, of whom Jim often spoke so fondly. Jim would always ask about my kids, who were growing up around the same time as Patrick. He wanted to make sure they had everything they needed since he knew I was doing a lot of traveling at the time. Management friends of mine at Merrill Lynch soon after Jim's death informed me that Patrick Dwyer, at a relatively young age, was ranked among the top financial advisors in the state of Florida for Merrill Lynch. As the saying goes, "The apple doesn't fall far from the tree."

Don Webber continued to advance, holding the National Sales Manager title at The Kemper Group and also State Street Inc. I believe Don is currently a financial industry consultant.

Chapter Two

WHOLESALING VERSUS SELLING

◇◇

What is wholesaling? For that matter, what is selling? Simply put, selling is a series of steps—a learnable process a salesman follows to help a person, company, or institution recognize what their needs are through a process called *probing*. This ultimately enables a salesman to fill their needs with his product, both fixed and variable, and later in my career, also included Mutual funds, Separate accounts,* and 401(k)s.

The difference between wholesaling and selling is that while they are both sales careers, with wholesaling, you are selling a third party, such as a stock broker or financial advisor, on the benefits of your product for *their* direct clients—which for financial wholesalers is always a form of money management. Some financial products might include mutual funds, annuities, separately managed accounts, or 401(k) and pension products.

Some financial wholesalers like me sell all of the above, while others might wholesale only annuities. Some financial wholesalers are in-house, meaning they work only for a particular wirehouse broker dealer, insurance company, or independent firm.

I am not sure how many wholesalers are employed as of today; when I started there were fewer than 1,000. By 2007, that number had grown to over 10,000 people of varying

---

* Separate accounts resemble mutual funds but allow the client ownership of the stocks versus pooling money with other investors in a mutual fund.

backgrounds and education. With that said, lately one sees a lot of newer wholesalers with advanced business degrees. Again, do you think you can sell? If you think you can sell but would not care for the extensive travel and frequent overnights, you might consider applying for a trainee position as a financial advisor or possibly an insurance consultant. Please feel free to contact me at www.KeysForSellingSuccess.com for more information.

I should point out that while I primarily discuss my career as a wholesaler—because that's what I did for the last 28 years—a career as a financial advisor is also a great choice and financially rewarding; also as an insurance consultant. I can state this because I worked daily with financial advisors, and I was an insurance consultant. With regard to selling, I am from the school that says, "Selling is a learned skill." You can also develop your skills by enrolling in one of Dale Carnegie's local classes as I did back in the 1970s.

You are probably already wondering what you can expect to earn as a financial wholesaler. This depends on your sales ability. Generally, in the beginning, one's salary or draw plus commission is upwards of $100,000. Some earn $250,000 or even $350,000—with "superstars" earning much more than that. Experience needed for these positions varies. Usually a wholesaler has spent at least two or more years working for a mutual fund company. Sometimes these young people are called "Sales Desk Partners." They assist the field wholesalers while learning the products, learning to make public presentations, developing their selling skills, and eventually working for at least a year as a junior wholesaler for someone like myself.

Over 22 years, I had a succession of thirteen "sales desk partners" and "junior wholesalers" in my previous firm. All have been successful in their own right, and most went on to wholesaling. However, one became a stock trader, one a teacher, and another returned to night school for his MBA and became a portfolio manager. You will be required to obtain various licenses including insurance licenses, Series 6, and sometimes Series 7 securities licenses.

How does one get started? The best avenue is to google the websites of a mutual fund or annuity company—for example, American Funds—and click on "Careers" to see what is available. If you are just graduating from college, you might look for an entry-level position. Other resources include such websites as Ignites.com and Fundfire.com. Both provide announcements of job offers from various firms.

Chapter Three

THE ROAD TO SELLING BILLION$ OF DOLLAR$ OF FINANCIAL PRODUCTS

One cold snowy night in February 1981 I found myself in the town of St. Albans, Vermont, near the Canadian border. I stood at the podium in the Owls Club peering out at approximately 75 wealthy French-Canadian farmers and businessmen, along with two Dean Witter Reynolds brokers who had invited me to present at what was to be my first public seminar.

I wasn't nervous because I knew that a "real" speaker, Tom Barefield, was flying in from Dean Witter Reynolds's New York City headquarters to show me the ins and outs of seminar selling and presenting. I had gained some presenting experience from my insurance career; other than that my only public speaking engagement was giving the toast at a friend's wedding. Initially, the nerve-wracking part was the intermittent sound of hollow racquetballs bouncing off the walls upstairs. We didn't realize this rickety old club also housed racquetball courts!

A few weeks earlier I had seen a full-page ad in the *Rhode Island Providence Journal*, inviting the public to a financial seminar promoted by Merrill Lynch broker Peter Kelly and Security First wholesaler Mark Tully. Mark ended up hiring my eldest son Tim to an annuity sales desk job out of college. I decided to attend and watch these experienced presenters demonstrate the salient features of the tax-deferred annuity. I instantly thought, "I can do this and do it better." Now, here I was for the first time in my life in front of a large audience.

I usually use the terms "broker," "stockbroker," "advisor," and "financial advisor" interchangeably. Today the term stockbroker *has evolved to* financial advisor *or simply* FA.

You can guess what happened. The VP from DWR, Tom Barefield, never showed—apparently, the corporate office had a more important event for him to attend. (Incidentally, Tom is National Director of Sales for Ohio National and hired my son Tim for a wholesaler's position. You will notice numerous connections—relationships—such as this throughout the book.) The result was that I had no choice but to conduct my first seminar myself. Thank God, the racquetball match upstairs finally ended. The response to my presentation was terrific, and we ended up doing a significant amount of annuity business. Of course, DWR Corporate's brilliant idea to invite the VP from the annuity company didn't hurt either!

I started believing that with practice I could make my mark in this industry with seminar selling, and I proceeded to do so. Very soon after the St. Albans seminar, I had an appointment with the number one annuity salesman in all of Dean Witter, Anthony "Tony" Nicoletti, and his Rochester, New York branch manager Ira Miller. Tony was considered the king of financial seminar presenting and published a newsletter listing his upcoming appearances throughout upstate New York. I learned that Tony had been a bank vice president when he realized the power of selling what he referred to as "tax-deferred CDs"— that is, tax-deferred annuities. Along with dates and locations for his seminars, he also provided tips on financial planning and estate planning. Prospects flocked to his events from all over New York.

In 1975, Tony wrote the first single premium in the state of New York. During my five-year career at Dean Witter Reynolds, Tony was also the leading annuity producer in the U.S. for DWR. Tony is currently managing director of the Rochester Management Group in Rochester, New York.

I immediately partnered with Tony and began sponsoring his seminars and speaking at some of them. I was amazed to watch Tony as he often took in checks the night of the seminar and set up immediate appointments for the following morning. My sales production started skyrocketing in my first few months in the territory, thanks to Tony, John Devlin in Rome, and Earl Catlin in Binghamton, not to mention the brokers: Sammy D., his friend Cliff Ball, and manager Frank Perna of Buffalo. They would always have a car waiting for me at the airport, and we would go to a local branch office for a quick sales meeting followed by a trip to the Buffalo Marriott for a two-hour public seminar. We did lots of business and had lots of fun, and this became a monthly routine. I might note that in the day, the Buffalo Marriot had the biggest cash bar in the entire Marriot chain. We would all relax there after our presentation that had 50 and 80 seminar attendees—without the attendees, of course!

Tony Nicoletti soon called an associate of his in Scranton, Dean Witter manager John Egan. Tony related what we were doing, and John placed an ad in the *Scranton Tribune* advertising a seminar, featuring yours truly at the Holiday Inn. Because the initial response was overwhelmingly positive, John called the *Scranton Tribune* and suggested they send a reporter to cover the event.

Three hundred people showed up that evening, and I noticed immediately that we did not have an easel available onstage. John spoke to a friend of his at the bank across the street, who lent us their easel—as PowerPoint technology hadn't yet arrived. Unfortunately the easel was old, rickety, and in poor condition, and as I was presenting, it collapsed. Manager Egan jumped up onstage and held up the easel pad.

I felt I was beginning to lose the audience, because as I was answering a question asked by a skeptic in the audience, I noticed that the attendee was not happy with my answer and was murmuring to those around him. I was writing my answer on the easel when I looked down and saw John's ankles and shoes. I thought, "My God, this is beginning to look like a circus!" Then the obnoxious attendee actually stood up and walked out. Thank goodness, I thought, that no one other than his wife left with him, and the crowd appeared to settle down. I still smile fondly when I think of the visual of me using John as a human easel that night.

The next day, the *Scranton Tribune* ran a story with a large picture and printed the entire seminar on the front page of the business section. Coincidentally and prophetically, Elin Pye, a representative from Mass Financial Services (MFS; a firm I would later represent), also participated in this seminar. (If you look closely, you may make out the brochure I was holding, depicting the old MFS Spectrum Annuity—historically the first variable annuity in the U.S.) Years later, I met Elin's ex-husband during a lunch meeting in Fairfield with Merrill Lynch. He told me that Elin was working for the famous Doug Wood of Wood Logan. Speaking of coincidences, Doug and his partner Scott Logan both worked for my future employer, MFS. To further the coincidences, when Doug Wood was National Sales Manager of MFS, he promoted David Milbury into the role of wholesaler—and David eventually hired me!

Opposite is the photo that appeared in the Scranton Tribune *covering the event in Scranton.*

The response to this coverage and article was overwhelming, and I had to stay in Scranton over the next two days just to help with all the applications and resulting production not only from the seminar but also from the *Scranton Tribune* article. The article also referred to me as a Dean Witter vice president, which I was not at that time. However, I was promoted soon

ANNUITY SEMINAR – Dean Witter Reynolds, Inc., 211 North Washington Ave., investment security firm, held an annuity seminar Thursday at the Downtown Holiday Inn. James Naughton, Dean Witter Reynolds vice president, spoke on annuities. From left: John M. Egan, vice president, Mid Atlantic Region; Naughton; Jean Briskey, operations manager and assistant treasurer; William Comerford, vice president, investments.

(Tribune photo – Olds)

300 Get Reynolds Tips For Quadrupling Money

May 8, 1981: The Tribune, *Scranton, Pennsylvania*

after and always felt that this was a "battlefield" promotion due to that article.

National Director of Sales Tom Peck called me to Headquarters at 5 World Trade Center and gave me the promotion. I was in the main conference room looking through the large windows at the Hudson River and waiting for him to show up. To this day it is very difficult for me to relay the feelings, the emotions I had on being promoted to vice president. Guys from another background might have just expected it, thinking it no big deal. My eyes caught the awesome sight of the Statue of Liberty through the window, and I welled up with tears.

I thought of my parents and how they felt when they first saw her and all they had to go through—having emigrated from Ireland to America via Ellis Island in the 1930s in the height of the Great Depression. I thought of the United Homes Housing Project where I grew up and how I had dangled from the tops of 40-foot telephone poles in frigid weather as an apprentice power lineman for HELCO. I remembered my fear of leaving what in the day was probably the best blue-collar job in the U.S. to begin college full-time in my 20s and sit next to recent high school graduates who were now freshmen. Why do life changes often seem to be such a big deal when you're going through them? Again, my mother's saying came to mind as it so often did: "Jimmy, will you just jump in and start swimming!"

The seminar I created was very successful for my brokers, and it was common for the attendees to bring in cash and checks. Once after a seminar in Watertown, New York, an attendee brought a suitcase in to the Syracuse branch the next morning while I was speaking to branch manager Bruce Brand. When the attendee opened the suitcase, we stared at $100,000 in cash as some of the bills floated to the floor. (Bruce called the local branch of the Department of the Treasury branch immediately, but the money was clean.)

While presenting with another wholesaler at a seminar at the Marriott in Newton, Massachusetts, an attendee gave us a check for $350,000, proceeds of a recent real estate transaction. The wholesaler was David Milbury from Massachusetts Financial Services, who always placed a beige blanket over the easel with a picture of the Nationwide Insurance Company's eagle. Financial companies needed an insurance component for the variable annuity, hence the presence of Nationwide. Dave later went on to become a mentor, boss, and best friend to me.

The client's money was earmarked for the MFS Spectrum Variable Annuity, which offered a money market fund yielding 15% tax-deferred. In hindsight you might think that you could have sold millions of a product like this; however, the obstacle back then was the "too-good-to-be-true" cliché (15% money market and no current taxes? It almost was too good to be true!). During this early era of wholesaling, companies like Dean Witter were just interested in getting the sale—as compared to a few years later when selling in-house products became more important. I began doing seminars three and four nights a week. My business soared, and after one year my territory went from the bottom—#14—to the #1 spot in the country for Dean Witter. I was to stay at #1 for the duration of my career.

Today, at least in the broker dealer channel, large seminars have mostly gone the way of the dinosaur. However, I believe they can still be orchestrated and will be in the future. Instead we began hosting more intimate, smaller types of seminars— what I and others referred to as "private client dinners." We began asking that clients bring a prospect, who could be a business partner, relative, or someone in a similar economic status as the client. We would buy lunch or dinner at a restaurant and have a conversation in lieu of a presentation and get to know one another. In the process we would try to find out the prospect's needs and financial experience. As with any sales profession, one adjusts and changes with the times.

Dean Witter kept giving me more territory, including New York City, Pittsburgh, and State College, Pennsylvania, and I increased sales everywhere. While New York City can be intimidating, I seemed to thrive. I really like the New York brokers; they were a little brash—however, they were genuine. I also had grown to like New York's vitality and excitement, probably because I spent so much time in my teens with my cousins in the Irish neighborhood known as Washington Heights. (As a teenager I would hop on the subway and go all over.) In addition to promoting seminar selling, I also initiated a lot of one-on-one selling with brokers and their clients. On one such occasion, I had just completed a lunch meeting at the DWR World Trade Center branch when I decided to try to obtain an appointment with a corner-office broker I will refer to as GR. I had learned very quickly that corner-office brokers usually don't attend meetings. However, GR was among the top-producing brokers in all of Dean Witter, so I thought I'd give him a try. Luckily, I was able to get an appointment through his secretary for later on that evening.

> *I have tried to contact those individuals who were significant in my success, particularly if the situation seemed confidential. There were hundreds, however, so to make this book a reasonable length I have limited the stories. Thus, unless I get approval, in some instances I will use a fictitious name or initials. The following stories are real, to the best of my recollection. They are also chosen with the intent of teaching by example and action.*

GR was a big man with a touch of an accent. I learned later that he had narrowly escaped death in his youth. We hit it off immediately, and while I realized he wasn't insurance licensed, he seemed receptive to annuities. Initially, I was slightly nervous because I knew his status in the firm; most wholesalers never got past his secretary. I also knew that I didn't have a lot of time, so I decided to try something different.

I asked GR to give me a list of his CD clients, and I told him to sit on his leather couch and that I would make some calls to set up appointments. (You have probably guessed that my confidence level had grown very high by this point.) About halfway through, I struck gold. The owner of a famous business on the Upper East Side, who was a client of GR's, agreed to meet with us the next morning. I met GR early in the morning, and we took a taxi uptown. After navigating our way through some heavily-armed security guards in the store, we were able to sit down and make a presentation.

As it turned out, the owner had six grandchildren, and we suggested that he move $100,000 in taxable CDs for each of his grandchildren into individual annuities for a total of $600,000. This was a lot of business in those days and also a lot more commission than on CDs. More importantly, of course, the client benefited from a better yield and tax deferral, along with some probate advantages. GR was impressed that we were able to bring in that business so quickly and easily. Of course, the immediate issue was the fact that he didn't have a license, although I was licensed and back then that was enough, on a temporary basis. It was important to get him licensed so we could both receive commission on the trades. He agreed to take the insurance exam and was licensed a month later—and I had a new producer and friend. At the end of the year, my territory continued to be a leader. I was awarded the Dean Witter Reynolds national title of "Insurance/Annuity Man of the Year" and also received a commendation from Rhode Island Senator Claiborne Pell.

Around this period early in my career, Sharon and I were invited to attend an annuity conference in London, England. In addition to business meetings, we were taken on tours of Westminster Abbey, Parliament, and various historic sites in the English countryside. During this wonderful trip we were wined and dined and visited more sites and medieval castles than we ever knew existed. We stayed with others at the Grosvenor House Hotel across from Hyde Park. Stars from TV's Charlie's Angels, Telly Savalas, and singer Glen Campbell were also staying there, along with the band Duran Duran. We met and hung out with many of them.

To top off the trip, we were given directions to meet at Heathrow Airport for a surprise "mystery tour." Upon arriving we were escorted onto a long needle-nosed airplane that turned out to be the famous Concorde. Within 20 minutes we were headed for the edge of space over Scotland. I was allowed to make my way to the pilot's cockpit through an extremely narrow aisle and actually looked up into space. Next the Concorde landed us in Copenhagen where we were welcomed by a band and a couple thousand residents who were looking at the Concorde for first time. We were quickly ushered onto a train and headed out into the countryside, stopping for lunch in an ancient hunting lodge, then more touring via the train. We ended the day with cocktails and dinner at a medieval castle in the outskirts of Copenhagen and were flown back to London the same day. This was only the first of many wonderful trips as my career as a financial wholesaler progressed.

CLAIBORNE PELL
RHODE ISLAND

United States Senate

WASHINGTON, D.C.   20510

March 24, 1983

Dear Mr. Naughton:

Just a line to offer my congratulations on your being named the 1982 "Man of the Year" and your selection as Associate Vice President of Dean Witter Reynolds, Incorporated.

This honor is, I am sure, well deserved and is a fine tribute to your enthusiasm and tremendously hard work.

With warm regards, renewed congratulations, and all best wishes for continued success, I am

Sincerely,

Claiborne Pell

Mr. James P. Naughton
50 Arrow Lane
North Kingstown, Rhode Island 02852

Chapter Four

MORE COINCIDENCES
AND HISTORY

Toward the latter part of my career with Dean Witter, management in New York decided that all their wholesalers should hire a secretary. I hired "Kay" who, unbeknownst to me at the time, was a secretary to another internal wholesaler in Providence—Whit Whitaker. Whit was my counterpart at Shearson; however, I didn't know him at the time, nor did I know that Kay worked for him.

In the mid-1980s when I told Dean Witter I was leaving, I received a call from George Clary, Security First District Sales Manager. (Remember my description of attending my first seminar given by Mark Tully and Peter Kelly? Mark worked for George.) George lamented that he had had to cut back his field force and that he had just laid off "JS" in Connecticut. He reminded me that I had given JS an entry to call on some of my Dean Witter branches in Connecticut and that he had done a fairly decent job. George wanted me to give JS a reference and get him an interview as my potential replacement, which I did—which was huge at the time because of my standing in the firm.

However, I had no idea that Whit Whitaker was also interviewing for my position, as Shearson was eliminating internal wholesalers. JS ended up with the position, and I believe Whit was given a small branch in Nashua, New Hampshire, which later closed. JS went on to become director of sales for a company in Hartford, and Mark Tully was hired as his national sales manager. (Mark hired my son Tim out of college to the sales desk of Keyport. You may recall that I first met Mark when he was conducting a seminar in Rhode Island.)

Later on, I told Whit and others that I probably, and haphazardly, did him the biggest favor of his career. As many in New England know, Whit ended up taking an inside marketing job at a sleepy firm called Eaton Vance, which began as Vance Sanders and which was the original wholesaling group leased by MFS. Almost everyone in the financial industry knows that Whit rose to become President of Eaton Vance and led the firm to become a major player in the Boston mutual fund arena as well as throughout the world. I often wondered what might have happened if I did not recommend JS to Dean Witter Reynolds…as the late radio newsman and commentator Paul Harvey often ended his program, "Now you know…the rest of the story."

Sadly, Whit passed on unexpectedly while on a skiing trip with his family early in 2008.

A lesson: When I left Dean Witter I received 21 letters wishing me the best and offering gratitude as well as references from brokers and managers. I learned yet another insight to this sales career. In these letters, no one mentioned what a great salesman I was—strange when considering my success— or what a great seminar presenter I was—surprising considering the hundreds that I had given. Rather, they all thanked me for my service. I will mention this later on: If you choose a sales career, remember that service is one of the main components of repeat sales. I always told my junior wholesalers and sales desk partners, "The best time to return a phone call is ASAP!"

DEAN WITTER REYNOLDS INC.
#2 World Trade Center, New York, NY 10048

JAMES D. DWYER
Senior Vice President and Regional Sales Manager
Northeast Region

TO: Northeast Managers

DATE: August 20, 1985

RE: Jim Naughton

It is a melancholy moment when I have to announce the
loss of our good friend and insurance coordinator
extraordinaire, Mr. James Naughton. Jim is moving to
a new job with more responsibility, bigger challenges
and greater financial rewards.

Needless to say, we wish Jim well, double well, triple
well--during his five year tenure here he rendered
service above and beyond the call of duty. His personal
combination of integrity, product knowledge and hard
work, plus a winning personality, were the perfect
combination to win the hearts and minds of the whole
region. Result: a whole new attitude towards insurance products, oodles of business, and a multitude of
Jim Naughton fans. In this case parting is not sweet
sorrow, it is pure sorrow.

Jim has put our region on the map in insurance and
his shoes will be hard to fill, but fill them we will.
Please be patient, we will find another quality man to
take Jim's place.

cc: Jim Higgins
       Bill Shiebler
       Phil Weeks
       Dick Hayes

ROBERT M. STONE (617) 722-3644
Account Executive

Dear Jim,

Since we both joined DWR about the same time, I've always considered you something of a Dean Witter institution. DW is loosing an exceptional person. I can't tell you how much you have been a help to me. Thank you for your energy - loyalty - patience - knowledge - marketing skills - and time... You have set a standard that your successor could only hope to attain.

Professionally and personally, I'll miss you.

Sincerely,

Bob

DEAN WITTER REYNOLDS INC.
One Boston Place
Boston, MA 02108
Toll-free Nationwide 1 (800) 392-6083, Home (617) 933-1535

THE HARTFORD

Paul S. Bosnyak, CIC
Vice President, Divisional Sales

1 Waterside Crossing
P. O. Box 320
Windsor, Connecticut 06095
Telephone: (203) 683-8158

October 16, 1984

Mr. James P. Naughton
Assistant Vice President, Insurance
Regional Insurance Specialist
Dean Witter Reynolds Inc.
42 Weybosset Street
Providence, Rhode Island 02903

Dear Jim:

A vote of thanks are in order for your great program in
"hyping" The Hartford and its' "Solution" to your life
sales force. It is not only refreshing but extremely
gratifying to see this kind of support from our colleague
in insurance sales.

Jim, I encourage you to continue to promote this creative
idea as I know it will result in a profitable relationship between Dean Witter Reynolds Inc. and The Hartford.
I look forward to the next update!

Respectfully yours,

Paul J. Bosnyak

PSB/ekw
pc: D. Drobnis
     S. Ellis

Chapter Five

MORE CHANGE—
MORE OPPORTUNITIES...

‹›

In business, as in our personal lives, nothing remains the same. Dean Witter was acquired by Sears and things began to change. I felt I had to make some decisions regarding my future. Northeast Director Dick Hayes thought I should consider sales management within the firm, which touched my ego. However, I loved wholesaling and decided to move to a company where wholesaling was their bread and butter.

During my early career with Dean Witter I was fortunate to meet and form a lifelong friendship with MFS Senior Vice President and wholesaler K. David Milbury. Dave and I traveled throughout the Northeast conducting sales meetings, seminars, and dinners. One negative to being a wholesaler/road warrior is the inherent loneliness of the job. Traveling with Dave meant that you would be subject to a myriad of jokes and stories and also lots of business, which took care of that negative. Dave was also very generous with his expense budget, particularly at a time when the budget of a "captive" wholesaler was sparse. In the evenings at dinner, Dave would coach me on wholesaling and help me get acclimated to Wall Street. At that time, as I stated earlier, I'd had no experience with either.

Dave knew everybody, and unbelievably, he ended up being the one to initially introduce me to the branch managers of Dean Witter. In fact, the second branch we visited was in Worcester, Massachusetts. Dave was friends with Jim Higgins. Talk about a relationship—Jim Higgins became President and Chairman of Morgan Stanley (formerly Dean Witter Reynolds). Jim appointed Bob Dwyer National Sales Manager. Bob originally opened and managed Buffalo, and both were very helpful early in my career.

Dave's presentations were simple, brief, and effective. He adhered to the "three B's" of wholesaling: be brief, be good, and be gone. In actuality, after I finished my presentation, I always asked for permission to visit with interested advisors and usually spent a few hours doing so, probing and listening. This was another important part of the sales process, where after the presentation I would try to ascertain the advisor's needs and the needs of his client.

I still remember Dave Milbury's introduction: "Hi, I'm David Milbury. I am your friend, and I am here to help you." And his close: "That's the product; now, what don't you like about it?" He also was, and is, probably the best relationship salesman I have ever seen in almost 30 years. His philosophy has stuck with me to this day: People do business with you for three reasons: (1) they like you, (2) they like you, and (3) they like you. (I am not embarrassed to say that I copied, mimicked, and plagiarized everything of his I could. Of course, he reminds me of that at least once a month.)

To see a portion of the article "The Five Factors of Top Sales People" on the importance of relationships in the sales business, written by John Asher (of John Asher Sales Consulting and Sales Training Company), look in the Appendix.

This idea of getting prospects to like you is part of the overall sales process; however, if a product, performance, or service issue severely impacts a broker, or any client, they might still *like* you, but getting the next sale is going to be tough. I don't think I need to mention it, but just in case: You also need to know your product and that of your competition. This is a given.

More change...I bumped into David Milbury, SVP at MFS (Massachusetts Financial Services, Inc.) on State Street in Boston during the fall of 1986. I was just ending a brief wholesaling job with a small firm, and things were not going so well. Dave asked, "So how are things going?" and I replied, "So-so."

Without skipping a beat Dave asked, "Do you want a job?" to which I said, "Yeah."

Dave arranged an interview with Don Webber, Vice President of MFS (Don had left Dean Witter and was now National Sales Manager for MFS—this was the second time Don was involved in my business career, and my life). Coincidence? I am not trying to make a religious statement with this book, but I can't, upon thinking back, ignore that mysterious email I mentioned earlier that said, "Coincidence is God acting anonymously."

I started the next phase of my wholesaling career January 1, 1987, for Massachusetts Financial Services.

College students and recent grads: I believe it's important for you to find a mentor and/or life coach. You need your own personal center of influence for your career and life advancement. Mine was K. David Milbury.

Chapter Six

THE ROAD WARRIORS: RELATIONSHIP BUILDING, SELLING

J ust like a lot of coincidences, you will read a number of stories about "relationship selling." Of course not everyone in the business will agree; however, relationships are a key to one's success. They certainly were to mine.

David Milbury and I drove out to Kidder Peabody and met with the late manager Bill Guerin and Jim Guerra in January 1987, my first month with MFS. All of Dave's friends quickly became my friends, which he also reminds me of every time we speak 20 years later. Jim Guerra was doing a lot of annuities, and we partnered up.

In the early nineties, at the time of the MIN (a closed-end fund) underwriting—which was the largest underwriting in the history of Wall Street—David Milbury was the number one wholesaler in the industry. I remember thinking, "He is a natural at relationship building" and "I am going to do the same."

This has always been a relationship business. Again, to do this job or any sales career you have to excel at building and maintaining relationships. These are some examples of how he did it. Events were moving fast, and I didn't stop to think about the process at the time; but if you see that something works—in this case, Dave's relationship-building skills—unless you're dense or have too big an ego, you do that same thing. Not everybody did, but as the saying goes, "Experience is a dear school, but fools will learn in no other."

While searching in a Barnes and Noble for information on book publishing, I happened upon a book on relationship building. I didn't read it, however; the price shocked me as it was selling for $140.00. "Why should I read it?" I thought, since Dave Milbury and I did more with relationship building than probably anyone in the U.S.

As I relate my experiences, it is important to remember that communications technology—laptop computers, Blackberries, and cell phones—did not yet exist. One stopped at a pay phone to confirm the next appointment, and I knew every rest stop from Providence to Buffalo. MFS bought us all Panasonic built-in/portable cell phones late in 1987 (which at the time meant a large bag, roughly 13"x 7"). Because the phones required the installation of a transformer in the trunk, they ran about $2,500. How did we get things done? We just did.

Dave was entrenched in the large Boston Merrill Lynch branches. He introduced me to the manager, George Cook, then subsequently Paul Ferenbach, District Director; Merril Pyes, Sales Manager in Boston; and Barry McCloskey.

> It's "coincidental" that Paul's first broker hire as a Merrill Lynch manager in the Midwest was Don Webber, fresh out of college. You might recall that Don was involved twice in my career/life decisions.

Later in 1987, I was bumped from presenting at a lunch meeting I had scheduled with meeting coordinator Alex Jackson in the Boston branch due to a scheduling conflict with insurance specialist Joe Gramell and Tandem wholesaler Chris MacLear. My cancelled presentation had been scheduled for the same day that a disgruntled broker shot and killed the branch manager, George Cook—a person who was well liked and respected—in the very meeting room where I was supposed to have been presenting. After that, I vowed never to quibble about a canceled lunch meeting again in my career.

My career had a nice boost when the Boston Merrill Sales Manager announced that I was the only outside wholesaler allowed in his Boston branch. This actually lasted couple of years. I used to kid that I probably had a contract on my head from all the other wholesalers.

Early on, Dave and I visited Merrill in Hartford, and he introduced me to Paul "Brother" Egan (now retired, but we still meet for coffee on occasion). Paul was not only a good producer for Dave and MFS, but also a terrific center of influence; and it was like having a best friend in the Hartford Merrill branch. Later on, Fritz Dahlgren moved over to Hartford Merrill (he now manages his own LPL Branch in Middletown, Connecticut).

When I speak of relationships, keep in mind that they often take months and years to build. I met Fritz in late 1981 when he took over as manager for Dean Witter Reynolds in Binghamton, New York. I also met Jill Packard, formerly Merrill Complex Manager in Hartford and now of the New Haven Complex, and Michele Perrault, the Stamford Complex Manager, Stamford; both of whom were extremely helpful in my early success in the Merrill system as were Southern Connecticut District Manager Dan Donahue and Southern Connecticut District Sales Manager Frank Sullivan.

Boston was obviously a major market for me. In addition, our home office was located there. Having said that, Connecticut was a gold mine for me. Maybe it felt so comfortable because Connecticut was where I was born and grew up. I am not sure. However, I am certain that I got millions in sales from my Connecticut clients. I was included in just about every major meeting and convention, etc. by Dan Donahue. (Dan would open meetings by telling his people that he won a national sales contest selling the most of our total return fund's new offering when he was a rookie broker in 1970.) Frank Sullivan had me participate in every major training program for hundreds of his new advisors. Former District Manager and New Haven Complex

Manager Fran Adams, whom I discuss in other situations, and Hartford Complex Manager Jill Packard included me in all their events. You cannot buy that type of sales good will.

It's important to note that as a part of my relationship-building tactics that I had at least two centers of influence in the smaller branches and up to 15 in some of my largest branch offices. These were advisors I could call at a moment's notice if necessary to get the "lay of the land," management changes, firm initiatives, who had recently called on their branch, what products were being promoted by their firm and by other competitor wholesalers, and who was doing lots of mutual funds, annuities, separate accounts, and finally 401(k). This allowed me within about 15 or 20 minutes to get everything I needed to make my way through that branch and to pick up sales. How did I create these centers of influences? It was similar to creating relationships, but it required more of my attention in the early stages. Some referrals were handed down from Dave Milbury—I gave these special attention. It was worth the time!

As another example, I was invited to participate in a large East Coast Merrill Lynch convention for approximately 2,000 FAs at a resort near Tampa, Florida. At the conclusion, there was an announcement inviting all of the Hartford Merrill Complex Advisors to a private cocktail party. Following that a second invitation began echoing throughout the convention hall for yours truly to also attend. Of course, this caused my fellow wholesalers a little frustration wondering why *they* weren't invited to *their* respective regions' parties.

I built on and expanded the relationships that David Milbury established. John O'Neil from Morgan Stanley and other Connecticut managers also brought me into their events. I attended a major Prudential convention in Atlantic City. Sharon and I were invited to Bermuda by Advest National Sales Manager Dan Mullane. Tucker Anthony, Hartford Branch Manager Frank Ruierman, and New Haven Branch Manager Michael Jacobs included me in their annual fall convention at the Equinox in Waterbury, Vermont (I still have the pictures of our falconry experience—see below).

As I mention often, the first stage of the sales process begins with the attention phase. Try to envision this scene: My hawk unexpectedly flew off into the surrounding hills. Later, as we were all beginning to board the trolley busses for the return trip to the Equinox, I noticed two things: a large shadow around me and a look of horror on the other guests. Apparently, unbeknownst to me, a ("my") hawk appeared in the sky and descended rapidly toward my back, landing gently on my shoulder with his huge talons just barely touching me. Do you think I got the attention of every Tucker broker in Connecticut and beyond?

These are only a few of the large events I was invited to participate in. There were many more where I was able to bond

Jim and "his" hawk at the Tucker Anthony (RBC Dain Rauscher) convention, Equinox, Waterbury, Vermont

with Connecticut advisors. You can surmise how easy it became for me to get "one on one" meetings with an advisor or a branch manager after these trips and conventions. I believed that I owned Connecticut.

It's important to mention the sincerity involved when I speak about the significance of relationships in this business. You need to have a great respect and empathy for your customers, whether it's Fritz Dahlgren or Dick Fannon, Wellesley, Merrill Lynch. It shows through to customers and clients; they can detect a phony or a user. I made it a priority to learn as much about their businesses as I could. They all have excellent careers, but it's no secret that most people couldn't do that job, because while an advisor's job can be lucrative, it's also very difficult. I have always appreciated what they do. It's not "put on" but rather a sincere attitude that I've maintained from early on to help them grow their business. I believe that most of them knew of my empathy and respect, and it's why I was always welcome everywhere I traveled or was assigned to cover.

We later went to see Phil Baler, senior adviser and branch meeting coordinator of mutual funds and annuities at PaineWebber (now UBS) in downtown Boston. As if on cue, Phil brought out a sign from his desk drawer that said "World's Greatest Wholesaler: K. David Milbury." Phil was great and included me at branch meetings, as he also had the job of branch meeting coordinator. Later while at Smith Barney in Boston, he was appointed to the same position. It is extremely important to have meeting coordinators as friends. It's even nicer when you really like them, and I did. I was blessed.

Relationship-building is an important component of the sales/wholesaling process. It can begin with one acquaintance or a first client and generally requires the wholesaler's extra attention, including follow-up on a reasonable basis with pertinent information that can aid the client's (or advisor's) business model. The salesperson might possibly host a private lunch or dinner with a home office investment specialist or perhaps invite a retirement expert to help cement the relationship, allowing the salesperson the opening to ask for a referral. Often the salesperson is rewarded with many referrals. The referrals often become clients who then in turn refer others. Over time, this process can produce many new clients.

In my first two years with Massachusetts Financial Services, Inc., I was wholesaling our parent company's Sun Life of U.S./Canada annuities, both fixed and variable. Remember the *Scranton Tribune*'s 1982 article and the picture coverage of one of my large public seminars? The brochure I was holding was one of their early variable annuities—Spectrum. In addition to wholesaling annuities, we were selling a relatively new product called Compass Life. This product allowed our funds to grow tax free due to a Life Insurance feature. I sold millions, and was the firm's sales leader of this product.

I should mention that after leaving Dean Witter, I exclusively sold a similar product with a division of Monarch Life, thus I knew this product inside and out. With the help of Tucker Anthony Manager Jim Hayes, we found a market with Boston Banks. Jim helped arrange a Bank Seminar at the Ritz Carlton. We had more than a hundred bankers attend. The obstacle to this product was that it, again, seemed " to good to be true," and it was. The IRS eventually disallowed many of its benefits and it finally got shut down. If you were lucky enough to purchase it, you were for the most part grandfathered.

This format for selling—i.e., inviting large groups of our clients, the financial advisors, to luncheon meetings at the Meridian Hotel—became legendary in Boston. David Milbury and I would often invite 250 to 300 Boston advisors from all the major brokerage firms. We put a lot of pressure on ourselves by guaranteeing the hotel a minimum of 250 guests. We also worked our tails off down to the last hour, running around Boston sometimes in the rain and snow with reminder flyers and phone calls, selling our broker clients to show up. And we routinely stood sweating, self-doubting, and praying at the top of the escalators. Why did they always seem to wait until 11:58 and then show up *en masse*? We always had the largest record-breaking attendance in the U.S. to hear a story or a presentation with some of our best portfolio managers regarding the salient features of new products that we were launching. I did the same later when we began launching our 401(k) program. You can imagine how this type of "group" selling would be the envy of any salesman. How, why, were we able to command such large attendance? ... *Relationships!*

Later in 1988, Dave asked me to join him on the mutual fund side of the business. I considered this a great opportunity, since mutual funds were the "bread and butter" of our firms business.

Next, it was down to New Haven to meet with the mid-New England Merrill Lynch District Director, Fran Adams. We asked Fran to help in our quest to get MFS to do a Connecticut State Fund (it would have been the second such fund in the state). Fran drove up to Boston on his own dime (talk about a friend!) and pitched the idea to senior management and miscellaneous senior executives. Portfolio Manager Peter Coffin, who was from West Hartford, also contributed some supportive data.

At the close of the meeting, Fran pointed to me and said, "Give me an MFS Connecticut State tax-free Municipal Bond Fund and give me C-shares, and I'll put this kid on the map." It almost worked, but MFS was afraid they would alienate the banks with C-shares*, and some senior management didn't think state Muni funds were profitable. That ended the possibility of me having a Connecticut Muni Fund but not our relationship with Fran. (As a wholesaler, it was important to have a solid, performing, competitive state Muni fund because that was what was selling in the era.) Months later, a Tennessee municipal fund was released for sale, and I thought, "What?"

This was wholesaling in the mid-1990s. Eaton Vance soon after launched a Massachusetts C-share Muni fund, so they

---

* *C shares* were a pricing innovation whereby we were able to eliminate the up-front sale charge by increasing the funds management fee and having a rear-end, one-year surrender fee.

ended up with a no-load—meaning they didn't charge a sales fee up front—C-share with a much greater yield than we or anyone else had. They owned the world at that time; trying to compete with their product was futile.

Mutual funds began attracting large dollars. Early in the mid-1990s, I brought in a consultant who had control of $150 million in airline pilot pension money. He presented his case to senior management and said he wanted to do what he referred to as an "asset allocation" (meaning to pick different funds and rebalance or change once in a while). MFS senior management was afraid of "market timing" (see below). As a result, we cautiously offered to take a third of it.

> *For those outside the securities industry,* **market timing** *refers to an illegal attempt to move mutual fund money in and out of a stock or bond fund and into a money market fund excessively, often based possibly on information one has learned that isn't available to the public. Often it happens with international funds due to the different time periods overseas. In 2003, it was concluded that some firms committed fraud when they allowed some clients to trade more frequently than allowed in their prospectus. Sometimes market timing is tied to late trading, whereby someone finds an illegal way of entering a mutual fund trade after the 4:00 P.M. market close. This is unlike a stock trade, which you initiate for a set price (i.e., $25 per share of stock). When you sell a mutual fund, you do not know the price you will get until 4:00 P.M. Thus you can see the illegal advantage of being able to enter "late trades."*

He replied, "No way," claiming, "*[another famous Boston mutual fund]* would take it all!" I cannot confirm whether they did or didn't accept the money, but the example warrants mentioning because it points up the large sums of money the mutual fund business had started to attract in the mid-1990s.

Moreover, our management was possibly correct: that this client's asset allocation program might have been the beginning of so-called "market timing." We will never know for sure.

WHOLESALING HISTORY CONTINUED

In all fairness to the newer generation of wholesalers, they will not have the opportunity that I had with sales contests and trips. In the mid-1990s I often brought brokers and spouses, along with my wife, to the Topnotch Resort in Stowe, Vermont, for a weekend of skiing and overall fun. We invited these broker clients to our conventions based on many criteria. This led to bonding and cementing relationships that in many cases have lasted for a lifetime. With the new regulatory era, which I will discuss later on, sales contests and trips are a thing of the past. This practice is common for most sales organizations; however, for the mutual fund industry in this era it is either banned or highly regulated.

Chapter Seven

HAZARDS OF THE JOB

M ost wholesalers and road warriors can relate to this following story. One of my first meetings was a breakfast meeting for PaineWebber in Burlington, Vermont. I drove to White River Junction, Vermont, on a warm spring evening wearing a fancy gym outfit with a pair of brand-new gray Nike sneakers. Immediately after I checked into the Howard Johnson Motel, approximately 9:45 P.M., I realized I had neglected to pack my dress shoes. Here I was with a brand-new suit and a pair of new gray sneakers heading to one of my first branch meetings.

I ran to the front desk, hoping to maybe find a mall within a short distance that had a shoe store that might still be open. There was a shoe store, but unfortunately it was closing in five minutes, and I was ten minutes away. I then tried to buy the hotel manager's shoes but he was a size 12, and I was a size $8^{1/2}$. He wouldn't do it. I headed out early the next morning for Burlington, thinking that I might find a shoe store that would open before my meeting was supposed to begin, at 9:00 A.M. The knot in my stomach got tighter. I was thinking, "My first meeting, my first impression, and all I have are gray sneakers."

No luck finding a store, so I decided to go into the branch, where I was directed to a cluttered conference room with couches and chairs strewn all over the place. I figured that with the layout of the room, as long as I stayed in a particular spot

41

the brokers wouldn't notice the sneakers. Before anyone came in I jumped on a couch that was underneath the meeting easel and wrote down some of the salient selling points of my product. The meeting began soon after, with good attendance. Later, in response to a question, I leaned over the couch to draw my reply on the easel, and it started falling—reminding me of the time back in Scranton. Without missing a beat, I jumped up on the couch, caught the easel, and continued with my presentation—only to note the look on the manager's face when he peered at my Nikes. Of course, I immediately tried to make light of the situation by telling everyone that in addition to being an MFS wholesaler, I was also an Olympic runner who had just run up from Providence. That didn't go over too well, and the manager grumbled, "He can do that once in my office—just one time." Incredibly, I got business almost immediately out of that meeting.

On another occasion, when I had just started working for David Milbury, he and I had been requested to speak at a lunch seminar in Boston—meaning clients and members of the investing public would be in the audience. I arrived at Le Meridian Hotel on Franklin Street where Dave and I had a private parking arrangement with Big Bob, the doorman, and his colleagues. It was like having a combo office/parking spot on the street in the heart of the financial district, with easy access to our clients. Dave was waiting and looking at his watch as I arrived at the hotel (he was always a stickler for punctuality). As I got out of my car, he asked where my suit coat was.

"Oh, ——!" I thought. I had left it at home, hanging on the door. Dave, frowning, escorted me first to Filene's Basement, where I purchased an inexpensive suit, then over to Luigi's Tailor Shop where we waited while Luigi tailored my suit. This all took about 50 minutes, and we were done just in time for the seminar. It's amazing how you can look back at the situations that at the moment cause so much pain. Now they seem so funny, nothing like the nerve-wracking feeling you're experiencing at the time. You might want to read the book *Don't Sweat the Small Stuff*; you will find that it's all small stuff.

I should mention the ribbing I had to endure from Dave Milbury and others over the black 1998 Lincoln Town Car I purchased. Check this out for coincidences.

I pulled up in front of Le Meridien to park the Lincoln. Within seconds of parking, my passenger rear door was thrown open and a large duffle bag, followed by a harried businessman fell into the back seat. Before I could utter a word, the uninvited passenger shouted, "Take me to the airport, *now, fast!*"

Of course, in no uncertain terms, I told him get out of my car, pronto. Now who would you imagine was almost directly in back of this guy coming out the revolving door? You're right, Dave Milbury. I ended up taking so much good-natured ridicule not only from Dave but from my kids—who called the Lincoln an "old man's car"—that I traded it in within the week. Even portfolio manager and president of the firm John Balen, whom I occasionally picked up and drove to speaking engagements, asked why I needed "such a car." (Of course, John drove around in a 1940s pick-up truck—I'm not kidding!). Dave didn't keep the scene or the story to himself; everybody in the firm heard about it.

What a great job; we had more fun and laughs and did more business than I could imagine in my wildest dreams.

Another wholesaler and road warrior problem is being a good husband and father. My children were growing up quickly. All three of them became soccer players, so I made it a personal goal to attend all their important games. I became an assistant soccer coach. I probably missed a few sales; however, there was no question of what or who came first.

It also helps to have an understanding wife like mine. The pressure on spouses and families in this career is incredible. We made sure to spend quality time together and took many family trips to Disney World, etc. I was not a fanatic golfer, but of course, with a handicap like mine, how could I be? When I came home, I stayed at home. We are still a very close, loving family today.

I continued promoting the seminar selling that had been so successful for me at Dean Witter and also meetings with our clients and prospects. It quickly became apparent to me that there were a lot of advantages to being an "in-house wholesaler," as I was at Dean Witter. Obtaining a meeting was a given; they had to let me in. Now, I was selling my way into the door.

I began the process of creating new relationships and building on existing relationships that David had cultivated with all of the wire-house brokerage firms.

In the fall of my first year with MFS, "Black Monday" occurred—when the stock market crashed severely. National Sales Director Claude Thomas hosted a national wholesaler conference call almost immediately and told us to go home and assure our spouses that our jobs were safe. He said that we might all have to take a small cut in pay, but we never did.

"We take care of our own; that is why you're with MFS."

There are numerous reasons why you would want to be a part of not only a good money management firm but one that is also a loyal, employee-oriented firm, one that takes care of your families. For me, that Black Monday story sums it all up.

Years later, I was being inducted into my firm's Hall of Fame for my sales achievements over the years, at the Cape Cod Ocean Edge Resort, Senior Management convention. I was asked by Human Resource Director Claire Muhm if during lunch I would be willing to give my thoughts on what the firm meant to me. The Black Monday story is what I relayed to senior management.

Nothing stays the same....

Business was okay; we were coming off a close-end fund era which caused us a little bump in the road with retail sales. In the early 1990s, I was about to begin a breakfast meeting in the Hartford Smith Barney branch when the doors flew open and manager RMC (a former Golden Gloves Boxer) said, "Stop the meeting!" He continued, "MFS is not going to do another meeting in here until they handle and clarify the funds they sold previously."

He was referring to the closed-end funds we sold; he wasn't happy with them and probably a little confused as to how they were meant to perform. I immediately fired back to my broker audience, "Hold on, don't move."

They didn't (I don't know if most guys could have pulled that off; growing up in a project probably helped), and I telephoned Julia Hoick, who was a quick study in closed ends for the portfolio manager. She and portfolio manager Pat Zlotin did an impromptu conference call right there on the spot. It worked, and everyone calmed down. I'm sure Mr. RMC couldn't believe that I was telling his guys not to move. Later, I took advantage of our late Chairman Keith Brodkin's open-door policy and told him what was happening. He agreed to try and do any future conference calls in this regard in the foreseeable future, and he did, and we got through it. It took a few years, and we learned how to sell under difficult circumstances.

I mention this for any interested college student whose attention I might have captured with potential of a large paycheck, along with the "All that glitters is not gold" cliché. If you land a position in the financial services business, particularly as a salesperson, it isn't always easy. This is true of any sales career and partly why one can make serious income. Suppose you land in the medical sales field, as my middle son Matt did, and let's say you are selling pacemakers and one malfunctions—or the line you're carrying proves to have defects. What could happen? What would you say or do? What if you just sold 100 cars that had faulty gas pedals? Would you do the most important thing a good salesman/wholesaler should do? What's that, you ask?

If you worked for me, it's a simple answer: Just show up! I showed up in the rain, in the snow, and when a product imploded—I showed up.

Showing up is synonymous with service. Remember all of the letters I received from my first wholesaling position? They thanked me not for my selling ability, not for my seminars, but rather for my service. Service is the cement of relationships.

Chapter Eight

THE ADVENT OF THE 401(k) AND NEW PRICING MODELS

◇◇

B y the early 1990s, Fidelity was making major inroads into the 401(k) business while MFS and other load fund companies had a 1% front-end sales charge—even at the million-dollar level—which made us all uncompetitive in the 401(k) marketplace. I also found myself competing in the retail marketplace with no loads (meaning fund companies, like Fidelity, not charging an upfront sales charge). In that era, one of my most requested "value-added" presentations was—you guessed it—"How to Compete with the No-Loads." (A load = an up-front sales charge, which could be 4%, 2%, etc.)

◇◇◇◇◇◇◇◇◇◇◇◇◇◇◇◇◇◇◇◇◇◇◇◇◇◇◇◇◇◇◇◇◇◇◇◇◇

Funds sold through brokers and advisors had a front-end sales charge, which was reduced by the size of the investment. Even at the million-dollar level there was a still a 1% charge on broker-sold funds. Fidelity now offers both. Many mutual fund companies such as MFS and American Funds believed that customers benefited by having a third party, such as Merrill Lynch, Morgan Stanley*, or other Wall Street firms, monitor their funds; thus, the sales charge helped cover the cost of that service. As a result, back in the 1920s, they decided to sell only

---

* The titles of these firms have changed since then to become Morgan Stanley Smith Barney and Merrill Lynch is now owned primarily by Bank of America.

> *through third parties. This decision created a need for field*
> *financial wholesalers to bring the mutual funds and other*
> *investments to a third party and describe, explain, and sell at*
> *lunch meetings, public seminars, or one-on-one presentations.*

More on the evolution of the mutual fund business: A few major events occurred early in my career with the evolution of B-Shares (12b1) and C- Shares. These funds did not have a front-end sales charge; instead, they had an early surrender charge, which helped us enormously when competing with no-load firms such as Fidelity, Vanguard, etc. SDVP Mark Warren convinced Keith Brodkin, along with some prodding from me, to drop the 1% sales charge at the million-dollar level. This occurred after I was asked to help sell a 401(k) to a shoe company north of Boston by Boston financial advisor JD. This was a million-dollar plan, and a million dollars was considered huge in that era. Pardon the pun, but I thought it was a "shoe-in" as the advisors' firm had recently taken the company public and the comptroller was a friend and neighbor of the late Joan Bachelder, who headed up fixed income for MFS.

Unfortunately, in spite of these connections, we lost the deal because in the mid-1990s at the million-dollar level, we still had a 1% front-end sales charge—and, of course, Fidelity had none. Around the same time, David Milbury was flying into Logan one evening and was being picked up by a limo from Boston Coach when he noticed that there were 20 such limos in front of his. When he asked the driver what was going on, he was told that Fidelity had invited CEOs and HR Directors from companies all over the U.S. for a 401(k) symposium at the Boston headquarters. They were in the process of owning the 401(k) marketplace.

The firm dropped the 1% sales load, and at about the same time, Carol Geremia was appointed as the New England 401(k) Specialist. Not all channels readily jumped on board, but I saw the potential sales with the help of someone as knowledgeable and personable as Carol. Together, we brought in millions, and the 401(k) went from almost zero to about 30% of my production. My overall production skyrocketed as well. As Carol advanced into management, she appointed Steve McKay to take her place, and our 401(k) business continued to accelerate. (Steve is now Divisional Vice President for The Hartford Retirement Plans Group.)

My lesson from all this? Take advantage of all your specialists, sales tools, assistants, value-added programs, brochures, and anything else that can help you make a sale. Sound simple? It is—but still a lot of salespeople do not do so.

I am discussing my early years to make the point that in sales one needs to make use of all the tools and people that are available to you. I had no "airs"—how could I? After all, I grew up in a project. I wasn't a know-it-all; I listened, borrowed, and worked with everyone. I tried to treat all of my assistants, sales desk partners, coordinators, and value-added associates with respect and dignity.

I also tried to get them to look at the fun side of their jobs like I did by sharing my war stories and downplaying calamities. I think everyone I worked with had many laughs like I did with Dave Milbury, yet we both did serious "land-office" business, as Dave would call it. It's interesting that the majority of my stockbroker/advisor clients were not only successful in their own right, but they were also fun and had a sense of humor. Former clients still send me jokes. My goal was always to do tons of business and have fun—and that I did!

Chapter Nine

MILLION-DOLLAR
SALES OPPORTUNITIES

◇◇

I soon saw another market open to me when we eliminated the 1% sales charge (load) for pensions. At that time, we also eliminated the sales charge on all million-dollar-plus sales outside the pension arena, referred to as *non-qualified business* (pensions are referred to as *qualified business*). This opened up another market that I called the pseudo-institutional market, which covered sales from $1 million to $25 million. *Institutional business* is generally $25 million and over. An example of the pseudo-institutional market took place in 1996 when a Boston adviser brought in a client who controlled approximately $12 million for a large religious organization. Their money was managed by two local money managers doing mainly stocks and bonds (this was before the *separate account* era). The entity liked the idea of having their money managed without a sales load and that it could move in and out of the market with a phone call in the event of an emergency. Moving to funds helped with their organization and management of their securities, meaning that they didn't have to keep track of hundreds of stocks and bonds individually.

It's important to clarify that "emergency" meant just that— this was not "timing money." Imagine being responsible for a several-million-dollar endowment fund that held various stocks and bonds and you believe that a market correction is imminent. It could take some time to sell lots of individual stocks and bonds. With the endowments' assets (assuming their charters permit mutual funds), it would be possible for appropriate endowment officers to move all of their millions into the money market at 3:55 P.M.—five minutes before the market closes—via a phone call to the fund company. This was the beginning of some the largest non-qualified (not part of a pension plan) mutual fund trades of my career.

This inspired me to put together an NAV: a *net asset value* broker presentation. I called it "Making Money with NAV Pricing." I ended up doing millions of dollars in business with municipalities, churches, colleges, wealthy families, endowments, and corporate cash. (For privacy reasons, I chose not to list the full name of my program.)

Sales creativity: I always felt that in addition to learning to become a great salesman, it was also important to develop a marketing perspective for your ultimate success. One of my large NAV (net asset value) million-dollar-plus producers suggested that I ask the firm to get a legal opinion on our government funds, particularly the short-term government fund. In other words, certify that they were acceptable for banks and credit unions, which we did. Next he asked if we could make a few minor adjustments in the management of them and see if we could get them approved for the Massachusetts Legal Lists, making them suitable for municipalities. The firm agreed and I did millions in sales.

Again, along with many other responsibilities as a salesperson, you also need to have or develop a sense of marketing—i.e., sales creativity. My middle son Matt, a medical device salesman, recently attended a regional meeting with his company executives, discussing the competition in a difficult economy. Matt suggested that his firm might bring in a great deal of business and gain some advertising by outfitting its salesmen with small vans that would allow him and his colleagues to provide immediate delivery to hospitals and other medical facilities of some of the smaller products at the close of the sale. This example of marketing sense gave the company a way of setting themselves apart from the competition.

In 1997, while visiting brokers in Portland, Maine, I—along with the new Vice President and 401(k) specialist Steve McKay —called on one of Maine's largest producers to take him and his partner to dinner. I said that I would not push any of our products, but instead would spend the evening helping him grow his business. I presented my NAV High Net Worth prospecting ideas along with the 401(k) prospecting ideas provided by Steve. He was the ultimate corner office producer, being in the top five for his firm in any given month and often number one. I was also aware that he was a very big producer at my biggest competitor, American Funds. During the next twelve months we received approximately $15 million from him. Not bad, considering I never promoted a product!

For a new salesperson, the above (in addition to being a sales success story) is also an example of the importance of listening and probing—i.e., trying to uncover and eventually fill a client's needs versus trying to stuff your products down his throat. Listening and probing, which are taught and learned skills, make up a significant part of the sales process.

Chapter Ten

NEW PENSION SALES IN PLATFORM BUSINESS

Today the emphasis in the 401(k) business is to get your funds placed on someone else's platform—e.g., The Hartford Insurance Company and others. It appears to be a more profitable way of doing 401(k) business for fund companies. In fact, due to this, there is now a new specialist career available, the DCIO (defined contribution investment only) specialist. Again, with creativity and a sense of marketing, I began doing what is now referred to as DCIO business in 1998. I placed one of our funds through a broker client of mine in the amount of millions of dollars in a major oil company's pension plan.

*Attention, college grads! There is now
another career possibility—the DCIO specialist.*

Another example of this, and the reason I encouraged brokers to prospect pension plans, was HF, who began his career at E. F. Hutton. Hutton was big on "coordinator jobs," and H got the Retirement Coordinator position in his branch. He gathered leads, including human resource directors and benefit directors, then stayed in touch with cards and letters containing items of interest in the pension and 401(k) arena.

Years later while in another firm in Connecticut, one of those "leads" contacted him, asking if he was still in the "pension business." The gentleman had just landed a position as a benefit director with a well-known national retail company that had a billion-dollar-plus 401(k)—too big for us at the time and too big for the broker's firm. Another firm said they could handle it, so H moved to the firm and became broker on one of the largest 401(k)s in the country. Fortunately for me, I was able to get several of MFS's funds in the plan. Again this kind of business, now called DCIO (defined contribution investment only), provided my territory with a constant flow while I did the regular wholesaling business, including hundreds of lunch meetings, dinners, and public seminars.

In July 2008, as we were announcing a formal move into the DCIO business, I received an email from a partner of a team in a Boston wire-house firm who concentrated almost exclusively on 401(k) production. The term "wire house" generally applies to the Morgan Stanley–Merrill Lynch-type firms, as opposed to such independent firms as Royal Alliance, Commonwealth, etc. His message was, "Jim, what would it take in production to make my partner Al and I number one with Jim Naughton?" What a nice ego boost, and what a way for me to log the first large ticket in the new DCIO product.

I replied, "How about a couple million?"

Three months later I received $10 million for the first multi-million-dollar ticket in the first formal DCIO trade. Wholesaling is like having a team of sales professionals working for you. I still feel the excitement of receiving these large trades today, along with the regular "bread-and-butter" trades. This is an example of the salesman having a relationship evolve into a friendship, and I was fortunate to develop many friends during my career.

This NAV marketing effort (i.e., having no sales fee at the million-dollar level) I helped develop culminated in one of the largest retail trades, excluding a pension plan, sold in the mutual fund business in 2000. I received a mutual fund ticket for

$40 million from one organization, a client of a Boston firm. I was given advance notice that the money would be wired into the branch one Thursday in October. By noon, about $10,000 had come through, and I became a "doubting Thomas." At approximately 3:40 P.M., after writing the whole thing off, I received a call on my cell phone and was told that money was pouring in. I couldn't believe it; I was getting a countdown in millions! The last chunk hit at approximately 3:58 P.M.—just two minutes before the stock market closed for the day—for a total single ticket of $40 million. This ticket and others allowed me to produce just $10 million short of $1 billion in sales for the year 2000. Actually, the remaining $10 million came in during the first few weeks of 2001 to create a *billion dollar* year for me.

Success leads to more success. Through another broker I was introduced to financial executives for a Midwestern state, and we were given the opportunity to bid on $50 million of state tobacco award money. By now, we were breaking the $25-million threshold of the institutional world, and it became a little political, because it raised questions—concerns as to who would get credit and who should control the potential sale. My suggestion was for all of us to work together and just make sure MFS got the money—we'd worry about credit and commission afterwards. It was exciting, however, at the last minute, and because of circumstances beyond my control, we lost the trade. You don't always win, but if you just keep plugging away, eventually you'll get your turn.

You might wonder what one would need to do well in the NAV arena besides a good marketing sense? One key point, as I related earlier, is to know one's competition. In the late 1990s, I lost a $10-million mutual sale for a church in New Haven. I researched the trade and found that it went to a competitor, American Funds. I called the ICI (Investment Company Institute)—the mutual fund industry trade group in Washington, D.C.—and got statistics. I then called the competitor and found that American Funds was doing millions in regular mutual fund business with pseudo-institutional clients—i.e., the church with NAV trades. Voilá! Why couldn't I? I now had NAV pricing, which meant (as already stated) no sales charge up front. I put together a plan that helped make me become "numero uno," not only in my firm, but also in the industry in some years.

I would be remiss in not discussing a trend that evolved in the mid-1990s: "value-added"—meaning providing clients with some elements of another service: estate planning, IRA planning, and marketing information. These programs were designed to help advisors grow their overall business. One might wonder how one can do business and make money with "valued-added"; just remember the first step in the sales process, the attention phase. With 10,000-plus wholesalers—up from 1,000 in 1980 and many having equally good performance—how do you begin to set yourself apart? It wasn't long before the competition attempted to duplicate our value-added programs, but I don't think they ever succeeded during my time.

Again, as markets and business evolved over the years, large tickets began to find their way into managed money, what we refer to as *separate accounts*, which also allow clients extra control, individual stocks, bonds, and some tax control. Therefore, mutual fund companies began developing products to meet the requirements of advisers and their high-net-worth clients. Today wholesalers sell mutual funds, separate accounts, 401(k)s, DCIOs, and annuities. Some wholesalers might choose to sell only one of these vehicles, such as annuities.

I realize that some stories can overshadow other factors in my success. For example, for awhile I had some successful performance in certain funds that aided my sales efforts and extremely competitive retirement products. They also downplay the ability I had to bring some of our top money managers to make presentations for me in downtown Boston. It's my belief that in sales, as in life, you only control what you can. You can't control the stock markets, and you can't control the performance of your investment products. You can control your attitude, and you can control your client prospecting and your client servicing, so that when your stars eventually align, and you have done your job and controlled what you could, you will get some huge sales and commissions. Sometimes it happens right away. Then you will look like a star, which is fine; just don't become what is called a "flash in the pan"—i.e., you lucked out due to unique circumstances and markets, and you use this single happenstance to carry you through the future.

While it's true that I worked with many major firms and advisors, it is impossible to list everyone who "made" my success. One such example is the Keator Group in rural Lenox, Massachusetts, led by Sheila Keator, who I first met in 1986 at Kidder Peabody in Springfield. With her sons Matthew, Fredrick, and David, Sheila was always my number one producer. She is also a member of the top 100 female advisors in the U.S. Excluding 401(k)s, the Keator Group produced the most consistently profitable business, mutual funds, and annuities in the northeast—ranking them among the top in the industry.

I want to be sure to thank the following branch managers for their support: Steve Lozen—who in 1981 (soon after I arrived at DWR) was hired from E. F. Hutton as manager for the Boston branch of Dean Witter Reynolds—promoted me and my annuity products at just about every meeting he held. He paid for a number of seminars with attendance of 100-plus clients and prospects at the Marriott Hotel in Newton, Massachusetts. Boston became one of my highest-producing branches back in the day. Branch manager Ed Sullivan, also during the Dean Witter era, promoted me and my products in a big way in Burlington, Vermont, and later Boston, as did his predecessors, managers Argie Economu and Omar Craddock (Stowe, Vermont).

Like any other salesman, a wholesaler has to sell something, create relationships, get referrals, and create more relationships—that's a given. Your life and job can become a lot easier if you can sell—convince—professionals like Steve and Ed and others—such as Merril Pyes of the Boston Merrill Lynch branch, Max Bardine of Boston UBS (Kidder Peabody), and Steve Brown, UBS (Paine Webber)—to back and promote you and your products and services. Managers can make your success become a reality more quickly than you ever could on your own.

Others who supported me include Barry McCloskey, Merrill, Boston; Chris Bean of Merrill Lynch in Quincy, whom I called on as a rookie broker; Gary Venable, my friend and Merrill advisor (and who was the number one financial advisor for Merrill Lynch in Rhode Island during most of my career); my friend Jim Joyce, owner of Harbor Trust Wealth Management; and Sean Dillon, UBS, my Irish Rockaway Beach buddy. Finally, Dick Connolly, whose mother came over from Ireland as did mine. Dick is a gentleman and center of influence and a great producer; everyone should know a Dick Connolly.

Bill Cholawa, Merrill North East District Director, was a rookie stockbroker when we met at Prudential, although many of my clients were rookies when we first met. Steve Anderson was often in the very top of all A.G. Edwards producers. I met Tom Butler, manager at UBS Providence, in 1987 at Thomson McKinnon in Boston, as well as Dave Dicenso, Providence, and the late Bob Gulla, manager, Kidder Peabody in Providence— one of the best branch managers I ever had the pleasure of working with.

Others included Frank Kale of UBS; Fred Gennelly, A.G. Edwards; and Bob Stone, Smith Barney/Morgan Stanley. All three of these advisors worked for Dean Witter/Morgan Stanley, where I started in the early 1980s. Kenny Zalcman, Smith Barney, thanks for the occasional $12 million trades. Chris Wilkinson from the Advest era, Pete Laird, Jr., Merrill Lynch, and whose father ran our International Department; Jack O'Keefe, SMB Westport; the whole Fairfield Merrill Lynch branch; Liz Angelone, Merrill Stamford; Southport, Connecticut, A.G. Edwards; Austin Drucker, Merrill Danbury; Bob Wyman, manager of the large Shearson/ Smith Barney branch at 53 State Street, Boston; Bruce Gregory, Morgan Stanley, one of my earliest broker clients during my Dean Witter days; Al Hammond, UBS, and partner Matt McLaughlin; John Guilmette from DWR days; all of the Keatings; Merrill Hartford; Providence Smith Barney; all my friends at A.G. Edwards

Providence; and my former neighbor, Dan Carney, and his partner Richard DiChiaro. I also remember Ray Rapoza from A.G. Edwards in Rhode Island and James Perotti from Morgan Stanley in Norwell, Massachusetts, as being great meeting coordinators and producers. I could list at least 200 or 300 more, but it's impossible to list them all. To those not listed, I thank you.

I had the best internal sales desk wholesaling partners in the industry, beginning with Sandy Horner in 1987. Terry Burgess joined me a few years later. Terry obtained his MBA attending evening classes at Boston College. He moved to Wellington Management Company as an investment specialist and was recently promoted to their London office.

Mark Mahoney, one of my more recent internals, was given his own wholesaling territory in Baltimore in 2007. Dave Jodka, who originally covered Maine, New Hampshire, and Vermont for me, was promoted to National Sales Manager at Schroder Investment Management, North America.

Some management books suggest that you shouldn't become friends with your support people. I can only say that all these friends and more not listed helped me bring in a high number of sales. I looked at them as part of my team, and we all became friends. (Experts are not *always* right!)

Over the course of my career, I had thirteen sales desk partners, many of whom went on to become junior wholesalers for me in my New England territory and eventually gained success in their own territories throughout the industry.

My most recent sales desk partners, Scott Matthews and John McDonough, were among the best. They made me look good even when mistakes were made. Chris Grant was one of my earlier sales desk partners and contributed greatly to the territories success. Chris is now an RVP, wholesaling for Sentinel Funds. Tim Chisholm was promoted to investment specialist/ wholesaler at Brinker Capital; Chris Logue, RVP, is a wholesaler with State Street Global, and Ken Davis, RVP, is a wholesaler for Columbia funds.

The father in me would like to believe that in some small way I contributed to their success, as Dave Milbury did for me. Dave Milbury and I both used a Marine Corps tactic in picking and choosing our associates. It's not perfect, but when time was of the essence, it proved pretty accurate. It was simply this: "In the heat of battle, could I send this person for ammo?" I will let you guess at the number of yeas versus the nays we came up with. Feel free to try it and see for yourself.

Chapter Eleven

SEPTEMBER 11, THE STOCK MARKET CRASH, THE MUTUAL FUND SCANDAL, AND RESULTING CHANGES FOR MUTUAL FUND COMPANIES AND WHOLESALERS

I was stepping out on my front porch when my daughter Erin called to me and said, "Dad, a plane just crashed into the World Trade Center." I recall thinking, "What an idiot, why would someone in one of those Piper Cubs fly so close to the city?" I drove to Exit 8 off I-95 to meet with Regional Vice President Rob Bonner. I was taking Rob to Merrill Lynch in New London for his first meeting after arriving from Michigan where he wholesaled and managed for us. Management decided that my territory, which was all of New England, was getting too big for one wholesaler.

I had associates covering northern New England for a few years. Ken Davis, who covered northern New England for me, did a great job. Kenny was promoted to his own territory in North Carolina and is now one of the top wholesalers in Columbia funds. I had also hired a friend of my son Tim, Victor Gillette, as a junior wholesaler to help with the regional firms. He also excelled and was quickly promoted to New Orleans, and then to St. Louis. (Victor is currently with Goldman Sachs in Texas.)

When I arrived at Exit 8 (10 minutes from my home in North Kingstown, Rhode Island), I noticed Rob standing outside his SUV, looking ashen-white. I asked if anything was wrong, and he replied, "Didn't you hear? Both World Trade Center towers are down; we are under attack!"

I immediately called Merrill New London on my cell phone, only to get a recorded message stating, "All Merrill offices are closed." We both decided to return home and be with our families. On the way, I recall thinking that it wasn't that long ago that I had called on Chris Ammo, Manager of the Morgan Stanley World Trade Center branch, and National Sales Manager Ray Anderson with Todd Crawley, who at the time was our national value added spokesperson. Todd is now a senior divisional vice president with Evergreen/Wells Fargo. I had set up the meeting at the request of MFS to do some public relations work with my old firm DWR; afterward, I brought Todd to the Tall Winds Bar at what used to be the Vista Hotel, where I first was introduced to Phil Purcell, who became chairman of DWR when Sears purchased the firm. I had also brought Todd up to the Windows of the World restaurant at the top of the World Trade Center. Now it was gone forever!

The stock market was dropping after hitting its high in March of 2000, and 9/11 made things worse. Growth funds got hit extra hard, and our biggest selling funds got hammered like everyone else. I still I felt that we could hold sales together until late fall of 2003, when we, along with many companies in the industry, got caught up in what was called "market timing"(I explained this term earlier along with "late trading").

We decided not to challenge the allegations and paid a significant fine. Some of our senior management were banned from the industry. It was not a good time; it turned ugly, particularly in Boston. Growth funds in general got clobbered—and almost everything I sold in that era was growth. The bear market and the scandal created a devastating effect for us and for other mutual fund companies as well. Sales slowed significantly during this turmoil, and it started to look bleak.

Next, we made the headlines with the supposed potential sale or merger of MFS by our parent, Sun Life of Canada—which kept repeating in the financial news. This didn't help sales and obviously never happened. Again, it's important to note: Often situations occur that are beyond the salesperson's control. What does a professional salesperson do? You show up!

In 2000, MFS entered the new world of *separate accounts*. Separate accounts in some ways resembled mutual funds. However, they are actually quite different in that they allow the client ownership of the stocks versus pooling one's money with other investors in a mutual fund. As a result, they provide some room to delete a stock and obtain some tax benefits. Thus they are attractive to very wealthy clients.

Bill Taylor, an industry pioneer for separate accounts, was brought in to set up a Separate Account Department and subsequently hired Steve Gesing as National Sales Manager. Steve, who was the "who's who" of separate accounts at E.F. Hutton, Shearson, and Smith Barney, joined us and taught me the ins and outs of selling this new discipline. Soon we were enjoying success with both large cap value as a separate account and included in the platforms of many of our firms and International ADR (both disciplines have fund counterparts). Separate accounts have also given us access to the corner-office brokers, as they are very suitable to their "high-net-worth clients," not to mention for those former NAV sales that I discussed earlier—trade unions, universities, charities, etc. We have also seen an increase in our mutual fund sales from these producers. As a result, many wholesalers have obtained various industry designations, such as CIMA and CFP. This situation is leading to another change in the evolution of wholesaling.

REGULATORY CHANGES

It is an understatement to say that we are becoming significantly more technically oriented than in the past. We are also more strictly monitored by compliance during this new regulatory age. Mutual fund companies have rules and standards for cash and non-cash guidelines, and each of our client firms has its own set of guidelines. One of my competitors recently remarked, "If you give a piece of candy to an advisor, you'd better register it with the SEC!" This of course is an exaggeration; however, one must be *very* compliance-oriented as well as being a good salesperson.

In the middle of 1998, an advisor who was leaving a large wire-house firm for a much smaller firm asked me for some support money. I asked him what he needed, and he replied, "I need a computer." At first I thought he was kidding, but he wasn't. When I told him I couldn't do that sort of thing (the cost was close to $3,000), he became indignant. Then he sent a letter to the firm, saying that I wasn't being supportive, and explained what he expected. This is an extreme example of the pressure a wholesaler is sometimes subjected to. In passing, I told the advisor to get lost.

I tried to support anyone who was trying to do business with me but always using sensibility. It was difficult for those of us who tried to do the right thing in the late 1990s before this regulatory era was the fact—there always seemed to be a few wholesalers who would give whatever was asked, making the rest of us look cheap by comparison. Now, we almost *do* have to register that gift of candy with the SEC.

Chapter Twelve

FINAL THOUGHTS

W̶e agree that this, as with many sales careers, can be a lucrative, rewarding career. What's missing? What are the
negatives?

You should know that in any given sales position, you are
the only one who controls your work ethic—i.e., showing up.
You are also responsible for learning your product; using your
firm's resources: sales desk persons, value-added components,
etc.; learning your competition's products; learning to sell; and
generally doing some of the other things I have suggested. Almost everything else is your firm's responsibility.

As I discussed earlier, if you end up in the medical sales
field like my middle son Matt, you could be selling a pacemaker
to cardiologists. If one were to malfunction—or worse, the
whole line turned out to be defective—you might find getting
future sales very difficult. If you were working for me, I would
tell you to "show up" and don't hide, because it wasn't your
fault. You might end up joining another firm, but your clients
won't be able to say that you couldn't be found. This also falls
under service.

Remember, I discussed *service* as a part of the sales process
and how my early experience told me that sometimes it's number one in the sales business. When things go wrong, as they
often do, service (including showing up) is paramount. If you're
wholesaling and a fund blows up or your firm makes an unwise

67

business decision, show up—you will help your firm, and you will help yourself. If you have to join another firm, then unless you move across the country, you will need to face your clients. Be up front, face the music, and try to help.

SOME THOUGHTS ON COMPETITION

As I complete my memoir, I feel obligated to mention a few thoughts on "competition." To this day, it's a little difficult for me to bring the subject up, as I was so disciplined during my sales career about not ever acknowledging the issue during my presentations, and I expected other wholesalers to do the same. I always believed that there was enough money out there for all of us. I also believed that bringing even negative attention to another salesman or their products was giving them a piece of the basic sales process. You will remember or you will learn that the first phase of the selling process is the *attention phase*. Why would you ever want to give your so-called competition anything, except for respect?

Yes, you must learn your competition's products, its weaknesses, etc., but it's all about your handling of this information that can make you a great sales person.

In the early years when there weren't as many of us wholesalers, I was able to convince everyone in New England that the real competition was not each other, but rather it was the "no loads". As mentioned earlier the "no loads" were companies such as Fidelity that offered their investment products directly to the public versus through a Financial Advisor. (Fidelity now offers there funds and money management both ways—i.e., "direct" and through their wholesalers and Financial Advisors).

I was so disciplined regarding the competition that I actually went a step further and referred other wholesalers to situations where I thought they could solve problems and satisfy clients' needs when I couldn't. I placed a letter from a National Sales Manager of a major firm at the rear of the book to emphasize this fact. It's a thank you letter for helping one of his younger wholesalers navigate the competitive Boston Territory. In another instance, I had booked a lunch meeting at a UBS branch in Peabody, Massachusetts. When I arrived, I noticed a young wholesaler setting up the lunch room. This young man went full boat. He was placing gifts of silver pens, and writing tablets at each desk. I also noticed his power point projector was showing Franklin Templeton Funds on the screen. This is a major firm, and I just assumed that this wholesaler (I will hold back his name) must have taken over for the senior wholesaler Jim Duryea, who I will mention a little later. I thought to myself, "Oh well, a double-booked meeting," so I prepared to leave.

Almost immediately, the manager rushed in and said, "No! This meeting belongs to Jim Naughton; he is the senior wholesaler."

Without missing a beat, I said, "No problem—this young wholesaler and myself have done a number of joint meetings together." I further explained to the manager that I planned on discussing a growth fund and "young wholesaler" is presenting a bond fund. It worked, and the unnamed wholesaler was very appreciative. That's how I handled competition. It worked for me, and as you read I did **billions** in sales as did my competition, listed below.

On a lighter note, I will share with you a story depicting actual camaraderie among myself and other successful New England Senior wholesalers in the early 1990s. A fad, as I considered it, was spreading through New England. Like all fads, they just seem to "show up." All of sudden we were being asked by Branch Managers and various coordinators to attend and sponsor what were referred to as Mutual Fund Product Fairs.

Often, they would be held at a hotel or hall near the branch. The advisors would invite their clients to come in on a Friday evening or Saturday morning when they would be able to walk around to various stations manned by us wholesalers. We would be asked to display our brochures on various funds, annuities and other topics, along with some of our firm's pens, mugs, golf balls, etc. Often the clients would end up with shopping bags, to carry all of our stuff. It started to appear to us wholesalers that the clients were getting more confused than educated at these events, but how does a wholesaler, who wants to be invited back into a branch the next week or the following month give his opinion to a Manager. So we just kept showing up.

One early summer Friday night, Branch Manager Bob Coburn, A.G. Edwards, Portland, Maine, decided he wanted to jump on board and put on one of these events. All of the senior wholesalers in New England, including yours truly, showed up, as it was a high-producing branch for us all, and it was the branch office for one of the most successful advisors in the A.G. Edwards system. After it was over, we the wholesalers decided to spend the night and have dinner at one of Portland's many fun restaurants on the water. It didn't take more than a couple drinks for everyone at the table to almost simultaneously blurt out that we would never do another one of these events going forward, that they were a complete waste of our time and our firms money and confusing to potential clients... also for road warriors who were out many nights of the week for our jobs as it was. We were all tired of trying to placate our wives with regards to the weekend overnights that these events were mandating.

We did two things that night—"we" being Joe Blair from American Funds, Nick Corvinus of Putnam, Jim Duryea from Franklin Templeton, Tony Robinson, Eaton Vance and myself. I think Jim Cronin of Aim Funds was there, although I am not 100% certain, and there were a few others whose names I can't recall. First, we swore an oath that we would refuse to do another mutual fund shopping event, especially on a weekend; and second, we all threw our business cards in a large bowl, asking our waiter to pull out one card with each visit to our table. The idea was that the last card would belong to the wholesaler who would pay the tab.

This was not an insignificant sum, but we were all successful, making good money—and no one really worried about the

potential expense. Well the last card to be pulled belonged to...
Nick Corvinus. Nick laughed and paid, and we went for after-
dinner drinks.

Maybe you will say or think that things have changed or
that competition was different in your part of the country. I
don't know about that, but I do know that everyone I mentioned at that table was extremely successful—probably some
of the most successful salesmen in the U.S.—and they became
and stayed so without having to "bash" the competition.

With that said, please feel free to "Jump in and start swimming!"

LOOKING BACK

My wholesaling career that I stumbled on in 1980—and
initially turned down—turned out to be the most challenging,
exciting, money-making career that I could ever have imagined.
I have only two regrets: first, that I didn't discover or find out
about wholesaling much earlier in my life, and second, that I am
not still "carrying the bag"—referring to the job of a wholesaler.
I loved it; no one ever had to call the house and give me a
wakeup call nor did I ever refuse to do an extra seminar or conduct a meeting on a weekend.

Even though I use my unique sales career as a wholesaler
to enlighten, inspire, and educate new college graduates to in-
vestigate a career in sales as a financial wholesaler, the basic
sales principles are pretty much the same. I have friends who
have wholesaled mortgages and automobiles. I also have had
friends who like staying put and became financial advisors
(once called stockbrokers), financial planners, and money managers. I know people who have been very successful in medical
sales, and there are lots of jobs in that field. The technology
area is constantly looking for good salespeople. These jobs also
have many different types of entry-level positions and other
jobs that are necessary to support the sales effort. I am finding

that in today's economy, you need to use that creativity I spoke of regarding selling and use it to locate these positions.

There are not as many job opportunities as there were a few years ago. Contact me for ideas—jobs were extremely scarce when I graduated from college in the 1970s. (Obviously, many things have changed since then, so I don't know how many of these would still be available.) As an example, I had a franchise route with Canada Dry. My job was to keep shelves stocked in an assigned territory. It usually took me a day and half, and the money was good. I worked at night for AAA as a dispatcher, often taking late shifts that weren't busy and allowed me to study. Sometimes on weekends I would take the 7 P.M. to midnight shift and bring my homework and a sleeping bag—I had probably no more than two calls in a night.

I was always on call for Budweiser, riding shotgun for the driver. We were usually finished by 1:00 P.M. and made good wages. Because of my military experience I was allowed to be on call as a substitute teacher in East Hartford and Hartford, Connecticut, even though I had not yet graduated.

The money and the experience were good; however, I had to schedule courses on Monday, Wednesday, and Friday, and sometimes I would take all my classes on Tuesdays and Thursdays to make it work. In the summer, I started a painting business and also worked on a main road in Cape Cod as a carpenter's helper. My boss said that if anyone stopped by and asked, "Just say you're a half-assed carpenter!" I also bagged groceries for a food mart. There is more, but I hope you get the drift. These may be tough times, but "when the going gets tough, the tough get going."

College juniors, seniors, graduates, and career changers might ask, "What can I do immediately?" Or perhaps their parents, who might be unemployed and facing huge college loans to repay, would ask the same thing. I would recommend taking some communications courses, particularly public speaking. Dale Carnegie (DC) training offers excellent courses in communication and public speaking. Eventually, once you obtain a DC

Diploma, you might also find excellent contacts, prospects, or centers of influence—people who, like Warren Buffet, are fellow graduates of Dale Carnegie. Look into business courses, including accounting and math; enroll in any investment courses that may be offered, if you can afford it; or consider getting your MBA.

Learn computer basics—they are mandatory to survival in today's job market. In other words, look for ways to differentiate yourself from the competition. Try to locate opportunities that are unique and not well known, as I did with wholesaling. Back in the 1980s, one of my largest producing annuity offices was located in Rome, New York. When I asked the manager, John Develin, why he left Syracuse and moved to a small rural area, he replied, "I am here because no other brokerage firm has discovered it." As it turns out, there was a major Air Force base in Rome, which provided a great foundation for business.

CONCLUSION

I stated early on that I wanted to present some sales career opportunities and introduce you to a unique, often lucrative career that might not be for everyone. However, one should at least be aware of the opportunity.

There are many varied wholesaling positions. As an example, my son Tim wholesaled only annuities, whereas I was a generalist. There are one-fund wholesalers, such as REITs (real estate investment trusts) wholesalers, and there are also institutional wholesalers. If you are interested, I will offer additional information through my website and blog to help you get an entry-level position—meaning, point you in the right direction such as a sales desk partner working with senior wholesalers where you will learn products and gain experience in different areas of the financial services industry.

You might do well by getting your MBA and becoming a portfolio money manager or product specialist. Or perhaps you might consider a career as a financial advisor for Merrill Lynch, Morgan Stanley, Wells Fargo, Ameriprise, or others. While earning a good living, you also will find great satisfaction in helping investors reach their lifestyle and retirement goals. Generally the training is free and terrific, and as mentioned, the potential income is also significant.

My son Tim took a sales desk entry-level job in the financial services industry after graduating from the University of Rhode Island with a degree in Communications. Within two years, he was working as a wholesaler and had success with the firm ING as the number one annuity wholesaler in the U.S. for Merrill Lynch Only division.

Tim is a contributor and a speaker with my firm, the J P Naughton Sales Performance Company. Many of Tim's friends entered the financial services business and have landed some interesting careers also. One friend, Mike Geraci, a BC graduate, lives on Laguna Beach and is a financial services stock and bond trader. If you have good math skills this also could be a very rewarding, lucrative career. Another of Tim's friends who grew up in our neighborhood, Jimmy Flynn, started at MFS as an entry-level assistant on my referral and was promoted to a wholesaler position in Texas. Jimmy didn't care for travel and is now a financial advisor for one of the large wire-house firms in Connecticut.

My son Tim, unfortunately, got caught in the 2008 market crash. His firm kept him on after laying off his entire division, including his boss. However, ING was forced to downsize, apparently due to aggressive annuity product benefits combined with the downturn in business, and finally had to lay Tim off. They have since moved much of their organization back to Holland.

If you recall, my story began in Ireland in the late 1920s and continued with my parents arriving at Ellis Island to claim their gold and riches, only to end up in a bread line due to the Great Depression. Some say we are in the midst of the second Great

Alliance Fund
Distributors, Inc.
1345 Avenue of the Americas
New York, NY 10105
(212) 969-2176

AllianceCapital

Richard K. Saccullo
Executive Vice President
Head of U.S. Sales

April 19, 2001

Mr. James P. Naughton
Regional Vice President
New England
Broker/Dealer Mutual Fund Sales
Massachusetts Financial Services
500 Boylston Street
Boston, MA 02116

Dear Jim:

I had an opportunity to see the note you sent to George Keith on the rankings of our local wholesaler in the Northeast.

In a territory that is so competitive it was a nice compliment. The fact that you took the time to send your note says a lot about you and your personal qualities. It is no surprise MFS is our toughest competitor.

Very truly yours,

Richard K. Saccullo
Executive Vice President
Head of US Sales

cc: George Keith

Depression; however, you might not realize it when you go to a restaurant and see the crowds.

I spoke with a prominent consultant in the restaurant business about this phenomenon recently, and he replied, "Yes, they may seem crowded, but instead of ordering filet mignon, customers are ordering chicken. Believe me," he went on, "they are affected by this downturn."

The same can be said of the malls; they may seem crowded; however, there is a lot more looking than buying taking place. The Depression is there; it's just not as visible in certain areas—and many people are hurting. Many are experiencing hardship and are among the record number of unemployed. Some are already lost, maybe forever.

Tim started his own business, a company that began with DJ-ing and has since evolved into a major entertainment company called TheFaceShow. He is now attracting corporate sponsors and has learned how to make mini-promotional/advertising videos to publicize his many events in Rhode Island and beyond. These videos also promote his corporate sponsors. Recently he has received contracts for events in upstate New York, Las Vegas, and most recently was requested to attend the famous South by Southwest (SXSW) Music Festival in Austin, Texas, performing at the brand new Key Bar.

"Coincidentally," the owner, Bob Gillette of the Key Bar and other Austin establishments, is the twin brother of Victor Gillette, whom I hired on Tim's referral as a junior wholesaler in Boston back in 1999. As I mentioned, Victor now wholesales for Goldman Sachs in Dallas. You can see that the connections and relationships are now carried on by my son.

What would you do if you landed a good job, got married, had children and a house, etc., and your company pulls out, leaves the country, or lays you off? You might collect unemployment—even, perhaps, some severance pay (although corporate America is not giving out much these days). You might move in with your parents or your wife's, if there's room. In my in-person presentations, I use Tim as an example for this possibility, and I discuss what he did not only to survive but also to thrive. (However, if you really want to get depressed, watch the movie "Company Man" with Ben Affleck.)

I have beaten the "life coincidence" thing nearly to death but consider this: My father, Tim's grandfather, started on Ellis Island in 1930 then moved to the Battery and breadlines in the Great Depression. He climbed out of that difficult time and became part of the new middle class. I also overcame some major obstacles, broke sales records in the U.S., and everything seemed to be great. Then *poof!* my son Tim and I both end up caught in the second Great Depression with millions of our fellow Americans.

For now, Tim is making a movie trailer and adding yet another story to the "down-but-not-out" long-term unemployment story and how he and his family survived—just as his grandparents survived the first Great Depression.

Both my blog and speaking engagements address how to protect yourself and your family once you become settled in a career. Maybe we can get Tim to give you a sample of his Face Show.

AFTERWORD

My blog is associated with my website (www.KeysForSellingSuccess.com). You can ask questions or get clarification on any of my topics now and in the future.

In the meantime, I will leave some timeless sage advice that I believe will aid any new wholesaler and/or salesman of any kind. Learn the basic sales process; make it an automatic part of your life.

- Practice probing with a buddy and become proficient.
- Force yourself to listen to people.
- Close, ask for the order, close often, trial close ASAP.
- Ask: What does the client need?
- Fill those needs with one of your products. If you can't, tell the prospect and come back again.
- Service, service, and service some more. Immediately after the sale or your presentation, have your sales desk partner call and introduce him/herself to the FA (financial advisor). Allow your sales desk partner to become an asset for the FA.
- Show up within a reasonable period, show up when things are great, show up when a product self-destructs—showing up is a major part of service.
- Return phone calls—*yesterday*!
- Develop your marketing skills and look for markets. Sometimes you find them through the competition; sometimes you will create your own markets. Research the possible uses of certain products.
- Leave the competition alone. Do not bring them attention, either positive *or* negative. Rather, spend your time on what *you* bring to the table.
- Adhere to your compliance rules and those of your clients.
- Empathize with clients. You may consider your job difficult, but FAs are on the front line.
- Be alert as to what is working, products value added, sales presentations—from your colleagues and your competition.
- Continue your education: I have taken four different courses since I retired.
- Split thanks for the business calls with your sales desk partner.
- Train your sales desk partner, make them part of your team. They are an important asset
- Use all the tools your firm makes available to you. Use your marketing sense to help develop more programs.

- Take care of centers of influence. Learn as much about their businesses as you can.
- Practice your presentations: at meetings, have a call to action—possibly offer to host a seminar or offer a hypothetical* to back up your product. Follow the "KISS" process: **K**eep **I**t **S**imple, **S**tupid! Leave something—a brochure or a hypothetical/legal report showing returns in past history.

Special note to college grads: Be aware that the myriad of entry-level positions in both the mutual fund industry and the securities industry of my era have temporarily diminished. However, with 76 to 79 million Baby Boomers retiring currently, there will be a lot of opportunities in the near future to find jobs that are related to this statistic with financial products. If I can help in any way, I will. Feel free to leave a message or request a phone call.

Finally, regarding my friends who became successful without a great deal of higher education: Please understand that this is not the norm. In this era, try to get as much higher education as possible. It will put you at the head of the line for more job opportunities. In listing a number of individuals who succeeded in spite of little college, my hope was to inspire those people who might feel lost because they were unable to attain a degree because of various circumstances. By listing examples of friends who succeeded regardless, I can show you that "Where there is a will, there is a way!"

This is not the end.
This is the end of the beginning.
Join my blog to continue this discussion.

---

* A hypothetical shows how a client's mutual fund investment would have performed over a period in the past. It is never a future prediction.

APPENDIX

<small>◇◇◇◇◇◇◇◇◇◇◇◇◇◇◇◇</small>

SAMPLE INFORMAL
"FIRESIDE CHAT" FOR COLLEGE STUDENTS

From notes I prepared for Mark Crevier's class
(Bus390 in the College of Business Administration)
at the University of Rhode Island

Want an inside look at a lucrative career?
Come take a ride with me. This sums up much of what we wholesalers do—that is, drive or fly to our next meeting, which is also how we got the nickname "Road Warriors." A day in the life of a wholesaler would look like the following.

The day before, I give you a short, scripted mini-presentation to look over tonight, and tomorrow we will drive to New Haven for a Merrill Lynch lunch meeting that we will host and pay for (I try to have three meetings every day, four days per week).

Monday morning: Because it's Monday, we will not conduct a breakfast meeting because most branch offices do not allow for Monday breakfast meetings. We have a 4:00 P.M. meeting at RBC Dain Rauscher and individual appointments with financial advisors in various other brokerage firms in New Haven, which is about a two-hour drive. We also have a client dinner (mini-seminar) at 7:00 this evening, so tell your girlfriend, boyfriend, spouse, or parents that you will be home late.

I happen to call only on wire-house stock brokerage firms like Merrill Lynch, Smith Barney, and RBC, but some of my colleagues cover the independent firms, such as Ameriprise. Others cover banks—i.e., Bank of America advisors. Different firms and different wholesalers often sell different products. (Some, like my son Tim, sell only annuities.) During my wholesaling career, I happened to wholesale mutual funds, separate accounts ("managed money"), annuities, and 401(k)s.

I explain all this further as we drive. In the two hours to New Haven, we have plenty of time to get you up to speed. For tonight, I just want you to get ready for your part of the presentation.

I tell you I am going to introduce a new fund that we recently released. You are going to help me with the first phase in the sales process, which is the *attention phase*. If you've not had any previous sales training, don't worry—we have plenty of time in the car to catch up.

For now, remember the auto dealership that you passed on the way to class with all the balloons and flags? That's part of the attention phase, which is your part on Monday at Merrill Lynch. I will have you write some numbers on the easel. At the top, write "**76,000,000**." You share with your audience that this is the number of Baby Boomers leaving the workforce by 2012–13. Then, while mentioning that these retirees worked hard and long for their money, write on the easel:

1. Don't want to lose it

and

2. Need a monthly check

You then explain that these are the two main concerns of these retirees, which our consultants tell us represent the largest exodus from the workforce in the history of the U.S. Say it with enthusiasm, and you will *have* their attention (the *first* phase of the selling process)! I also bring some "value-added" pieces, such as "stretch IRAs" that they can download off the firm's website or from our value-added website (we are always selling and bringing customers to us through various means).

Having their attention, I will offer a solution (product, mutual fund, annuity, or a separated account) to fill their client's needs.

We are now in a position to pivot to another product (which might have a "sister version" of the fund) in the separate account program in Merrill Lynch's Consults program. This program allows a wealthy client additional ownership benefits and also gives me approximately ten minutes to introduce and sell our new fund offering. Next, we ask permission to visit with each meeting attendee in their offices. I often request a show of hands from those who are interested in having us stop by.

Later on, at the client dinner meeting or public seminar, I briefly let everyone know the history of our firm. I will then discuss some of our programs and why we sell only through third-party firms like Merrill. I always use stories to sell my firm, our products, and me.

In the car on the way home, around 10:00 P.M., we can listen to motivational speaker Tony Robbins or selling techniques from the master salesman Tom Hopkins. Unless you majored in salesmanship in college, which most of us haven't, you're going to have to learn on the job. This is a typical day in the life of a financial wholesaler.

Could you do this job? Do you think you could sell? Could you do this after spending two years in a mutual fund company's training program? What in your life or college experience tells you that you can?

What motivates you? Money? That's great, but it can't be the only reason. I mentioned earlier that you could earn $125,000 to $150,000 starting out (after 2+ years of home office training) in the field in your assigned territory—and if you're very successful, three or four times that, not to mention the sales management opportunities. Many people think one has to be a brain surgeon or nuclear engineer to earn that kind of money. If that's what you want, terrific! But read on, because no matter what you do, you will still need to learn how to sell yourself.

SOME MEMORABLE
JOHN W. ASHER STATISTICS

Consider these two statistics about business-to-business sales:

- Four percent of the sales people in the U.S. sell 94 percent of the goods and services, according to two meta studies—one by Harvard University and one from the Gallup Organization.

   —From http://EzineArticles.com/460279

- Eighty percent of business-to-business (B2B) transactions are the result of relationships/consulting type sales, where the buyer has to like, trust, and get along with the seller, according to current surveys done by "Selling Power" and "Sales and Marketing Management" magazines. (Twenty percent are commodity sales where price is the driving factor. Today, in some industries, nearly all sales are commodity-based.) The statistics tell the story: Selling yourself is the most important sale in 80 percent of the B2B sales.

   —From EnzineArticles.com
   Jan 30, 2011; Asher, John W.
   "Attention CEOs: The Five Factors of Top Salespeople"
   John Asher Sales Consulting and Sales Training Firm

The Naughton family: Top: Matthew, Timothy, Jim;
Bottom: Erin, Sharon

Our grandchildren: Left to right: Sam (age 7), Jack (age 8),
Cole (age 7); Parents: Tim and Cristina Naughton

One of dozens of golf tournaments I sponsored; however, one of only a few that I actually played in. Left to right: Chris Logue, my sales associate, now a wholesaler for State Street Global; David Hanlon, financial advisor at Merrill Lynch's Boston branch; "golf pro" Jim Naughton; and Mark Joyce, financial advisor at Merrill Lynch's Boston branch.

Left to right: David Milbury, former Senior Vice President;
Jim Naughton; and Don Webber, former MFS National Sales Manager.

Left to right: Tom Peck, former National Sales Director, Insurance and Annu-
ities, Dean Witter Reynolds. Tom joined MFS as a Regional Vice President in
Colorado in the mid-1990s; Jim Naughton; and Don Webber, former MFS
National Sales Manager. Both of these pictures were taken at the MFS Sales
Conference at one the many castles in Vienna, Austria.

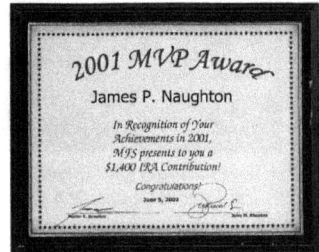

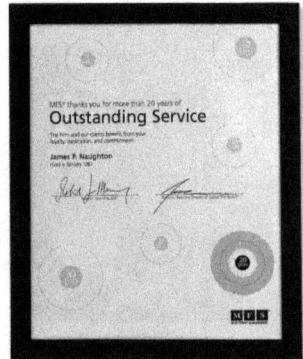

*Some of my Number One Producer and MVP awards
and my 1999 induction into the Hall of Fame.*

Clockwise from top: 18 years of cups for being among the highest producers of my firm; Number One Producer, 1995—The bowl for the number one producer was replaced with Rolex watches in later years. In addition to the Silver Bowl, I recevied three Rolex watches during my 20-year career; Enlarged version of the Top Producers cup (as shown above) awarded in 2007, my last full year in the field; Prestigious Chairman's Club member's mug; the Lapis Globe, a Heritage award for being a team player.

For purchasers of the paperback version of this book:

FREE Supplemental College Job and Career Guide

No cost, other than postage. US Postage cost = $1.50,
International =$4.09** (based on one book.)
Mail a return address and a copy of your book purchase receipt,
along with your postage check made payable to
JP NAUGHTON SALES PERFORMANCE COMPANY at:

James P. Naughton
51 Gosnold Road
North Kingstown, RI 02852

**Please email me for any questions you may have or if ordering more
than one guide book for postage cost for US or other.
Email - *info@keypublishingcompany.com*

More information may be found at
http://keypublishingcompany.com/supplemental-guide.html
(ebook purchasers, please refer to the web page)

Also by James P. Naughton:

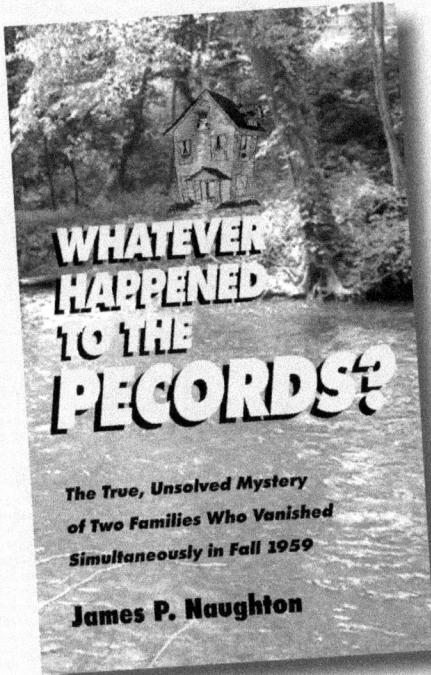

"A teenage true life mystery story of a family that went missing. Food on the table, pots on the stove; gone forever as far as me and my buddies could tell in '59.

"Instead of calling the police, I called two buddies to do our own investigation and nearly got killed."

WHATEVER HAPPENED TO THE PECORDS? is now available at *www.Amazon.com* in paperback and eBook, Preview it at *www.KeyPublishingCompany.com.*

The sequel to *Jump In and Start Swimming:*

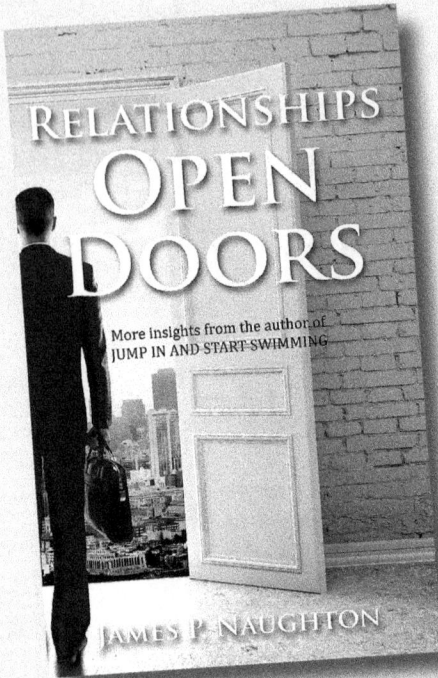

RELATIONSHIPS
OPEN
DOORS

More insights from the author of
JUMP IN AND START SWIMMING

JAMES P. NAUGHTON

"If you want to become an excellent marksman, watch, observe and emulate an expert."

Neurolinguistcs

If you want to become a top salesperson, watch, observe, and emulate the Billion Dollar Salesman, James P. Naughton. In this book, Naughton uses personal anecdotes from his $3,000,000,000 selling career to illustrate how much difference a personal commitment to his clients has made, and to point out ways to apply his experiences to your own sales career.

www.ingramcontent.com/pod-product-compliance
Lightning Source LLC
Chambersburg PA
CBHW060944040426
42445CB00011B/995